Tremé

GEOGRAPHIES OF JUSTICE AND SOCIAL TRANSFORMATION

Tremé

RACE AND PLACE IN A
NEW ORLEANS NEIGHBORHOOD

MICHAEL E. CRUTCHER JR.

THE UNIVERSITY OF GEORGIA PRESS
Athens & London

© 2010 by the University of Georgia Press
Athens, Georgia 30602
www.ugapress.org
All rights reserved
Designed by Walton Harris
Set in 10/13 Minion Pro

Printed digitally in the United States of America

Library of Congress Cataloging-in-Publication Data

Crutcher, Michael Eugene, 1969–
Tremé : race and place in a New Orleans neighborhood /
Michael E. Crutcher Jr.
    p.   cm. — (Geographies of justice and social
transformation ; 5)
Includes bibliographical references and index.
ISBN-13: 978-0-8203-3594-0 (hbk. : alk. paper)
ISBN-10: 0-8203-3594-0 (hbk. : alk. paper)
ISBN-13: 978-0-8203-3595-7 (pbk. : alk. paper)
ISBN-10: 0-8203-3595-9 (pbk. : alk. paper)
1. African American neighborhoods—Louisiana—New
Orleans. 2. Community development—Louisiana—New
Orleans. 3. Community life—Louisiana—New Orleans.
4. Urban policy—Louisiana—New Orleans. 5. African
Americans—Louisiana—New Orleans—Social conditions.
6. African Americans—Race identity—Louisiana—New
Orleans. I. Title.
HN80.N45C78 2010
307.3'36208996073076335—dc22   2010029556

British Library Cataloging-in-Publication Data available

CONTENTS

PREFACE

In the summer of 1992, prior to my senior year at the University of Kentucky, I found myself in Baton Rouge on the campus of Louisiana State University. I was participating in a program, sponsored by the Association of American Geographers, designed to encourage "talented minority and disadvantaged students" to pursue graduate degrees in geography. As in most academic disciplines, geography faculties have been overwhelmingly white and predominantly male. In some fields, however, such as sociology, social work, and education, African Americans have a significant faculty presence. Geography—and in particular, cultural geography—not only lags those fields in terms of African American faculty representation but is burdened by a disciplinary history that has supported racist science, policies, and practices, most notably in its contributions to the philosophy of environmental determinism. The importance of those issues has been magnified as human geography and other social science and humanities fields have become increasingly "critical" (that is, engaged in lines of inquiry into the production and reproduction of various inequalities, such as race, class, and gender/sexuality). Consequently, geographers have sought to increase the field's diversity since the 1970s. The summer institute program of the 1990s was one such effort.

While my participation in the summer program steered me toward a career in academia and eventually an interest in New Orleans, the basis for my critical approach to urban issues comes from my upbringing. I grew up during the 1970s and 1980s in a lower-middle-class black family in Lexington, Kentucky. Although Lexington had fewer than 250,000 people, it was clearly urban, especially when compared to the surrounding counties. The city's racial geographies were plainly visible; African Americans lived almost exclusively on the north side of town. Indeed, "the North Side" was a local metaphor for black population in the same way that "urban" is now a metaphor for blackness. In Lexington, I observed racialized spatial practices in action on a daily basis, most visibly in residential segregation and public school busing.

I experienced this de facto segregated experience largely from the outside because I did not live on the North Side or attend black schools. Occasional trips to the barbershop and various Baptist churches were the extent of my experiences in black Lexington until high school, when I began driving to the neighborhoods where my black friends lived. I came to understand the causes and implications of Lexington's racial geographies very early. Both of my parents grew up in small Kentucky towns in the 1950s and attended college during the civil rights movement. Even when my siblings and I were very young, my parents communicated to us the clear links between being black and enduring prejudice, bigotry, and economic and social inequalities.

In college I majored in geography and minored in African American studies. Of all the courses I took, human geography classes most resembled the high-school social studies classes I had found so interesting, while the African American studies courses fed my interest in the black experience and identity. In both fields, African Americans were understandably but incompletely written about in an urban context. To unite my two interests, I chose to focus on urban geography. The city seemed to be the area where I could most naturally study the experience of African Americans, the group to which I belong and which I yearned to understand better.

The spring semester of my junior year, I applied to the American Association of Geographers' summer program in hopes of being placed at New York City's Hunter College. Of the available locations, the New York program seemed the natural choice for my urban interests. Evidently, however, the prospect of spending the summer in Manhattan appealed to all the applicants. Because of the lack of space at Hunter, I was placed at Louisiana State. There, the focus would be on human-environment relations, particularly on the interaction of people with the natural environment of South Louisiana, including the Mississippi River and Louisiana coastal lowlands. At the time, I had no interest in South Louisiana or environmental concerns. Little did I know how fascinating I would find the interdependence of the region's human and physical worlds or how those relationships would eventually influence my research.

My initial disappointment at being placed in Baton Rouge quickly dissipated as the program participants began a fast-paced immersion in both the physiographic and cultural-historical workings of South Louisiana. The institute tacked back and forth between physical geography topics, such as marshes, erosion and deposition, and levees, and cultural-historical discussions of Huey Long, slavery, and the Louisiana Purchase. We quickly came to understand that in South Louisiana, the natural environment and human world had long been intertwined. All of this information was reinforced by field trips to barrier islands, museums, petrochemical plants, and sugarcane plantations.

The most anticipated field trip of the summer was to New Orleans, where we theorized about the linkages between the city's soggy soils and the practice of aboveground burials and witnessed the cracked sidewalks and exposed foundations that resulted from the shrinking of underlying organic matter. The moment of the trip that ultimately led to this book was a National Park Service–led tour to Congo Square, Louis Armstrong Park, and the Tremé neighborhood. I recall very few specifics from that tour. We undoubtedly learned of the slum clearance and urban renewal projects that led to Armstrong Park's eventual creation; we may also have discussed the impact of Interstate 10 on Tremé. Although that day's tour came closest to my urban research interests, several years would pass before I began focusing on the neighborhood.

At the summer's end, I returned to Kentucky for my senior year. One year later I was back at Louisiana State to begin graduate studies in geography. After writing a master's thesis on public housing, I chose to remain in Baton Rouge for my doctorate. I was determined to choose a dissertation project that would have me in New Orleans as much as possible. My adviser, one of the principal organizers of the summer institute, suggested that I investigate Louis Armstrong Park. He recalled how out of place the park seemed and knew an interesting story must be involved. I heeded his advice. The project began as a typical policy-driven urban study but necessarily asked some basic geography questions, most notably regarding areal differentiation — Why do some places differ from others, and how does that difference come to be? Underlying these simple questions are assumptions — namely, that near places should be alike one another. I was also committed to a study that was "critical." Critical geographies go beyond the literal meaning of the discipline to write or describe the world. In short, critical human geographies seek to understand how places, spaces, and landscapes are the products of uneven power relationships. Furthermore, critical geographies attempt to comprehend how the lives of those not in power are governed in those spaces and how those people resist their oppression.

I undertook the study of Louis Armstrong Park after being immersed for two years in the public housing literature. I was largely unaware that during that time (1993–96), scholars had begun to examine the nature of public spaces. The trend began in the late 1980s with urban scholars critiquing the general "disappearance" or "erosion" of public space. More specifically, questions were being asked about the transition of public spaces from being open and accessible publicly owned areas to those that catered to private business interests or the concerns of middle-class citizens, with both processes assisted by local governments.[1] The development of this new scholarship grew from a critique of Jürgen Habermas's ideas about the bourgeois public sphere and the application of theories developed by Henri Lefebvre, David Harvey, Manuel Castells, and others about the structure and workings of cities.[2] Much of this new literature focused on the policing of these public spaces to exclude what became known as the nonconsuming public — that is, the poor, the homeless, ethnic and racial minorities, and children. Although public space took on its own identity as an area of study, many of the writings on the topic were part of a larger literature on the postmodern or poststructural city.[3]

I began writing about Armstrong Park in the context of this public space literature, only to find out that the park did not neatly fit into discussions about exclusion and privatization. I soon discovered that the real story of Louis Armstrong Park was the story of the surrounding neighborhood, Faubourg Tremé. Although not formal public spaces in the sense of parks or atria, neighborhoods such as Tremé fit into the prevailing public space discourse as oppositional communities, places where those excluded from the bourgeois public sphere (and thus public space) resided and that they made their own. Nancy Fraser refers to these spaces as subaltern counterpublics, while bell hooks, writing specifically about African Americans, uses the term *homeplace*.[4] Regardless of terminology, these places were understood to serve as spaces of resistance and the basis for identity. Tremé, with its civic institutions and parading traditions, had been a counterpublic for nearly two centuries. I thus began to write about Tremé as an oppositional, counterspace community. I also drew on important changes taking place in the scholarly writing about African American communities and cultural landscapes.

For much of the twentieth century, writings about African Americans focused on where they lived and their levels of isolation or lack of assimilation. Beginning in the late 1960s, a time of increasing disinvestment in inner-city communities and heightened racial tensions, scholars paid significant attention to the ills plaguing African Americans living in ghettos. Writing in this style came to be called the "ghetto synthesis" or "pathological ghetto" model. Research that focused on more positive aspects of black urban life was commonly concerned with the experiences of black elites, such as owners of insurance companies and newspapers. The fascination with elites was likely based on an assimilationist logic that sought to identify aspects of black life on par with white achievements. In addition, research on black elites was likely driven by the availability of public records.

By the early 1970s, in the midst of work on the ghetto, scholars began criticizing this approach. In 1973, John Blassingame wrote, "When . . . scholars attempt to study the black community from the inside, focus on people rather than solely on real estate, analyze black hopes as well as black frustrations, and the solutions blacks proposed as well as the problems they faced, we will begin to understand the impact of urbanization on blacks. We need to know as much about black dreams as we do about white fears of blacks, as much about black institutions as housing patterns, black occupations as unemployment and black successes as black failures."[5]

Blassingame's comments come as no surprise in light of the fact that he had just published a book on black New Orleans that highlighted the richness of the community's institutions and achievements.[6] With few exceptions, however, calls for change went unanswered until the late 1980s and early 1990s, when scholars began to focus on the ways that, even under slavery and Jim Crow, working-class African Americans possessed complex familial and communal networks and resisted oppression. In the words of K. W. Goings and R. A. Mohl, this new agency-centered research "conveys a sense of active involvement, of people empowered, engaged in struggle, living their lives, and shaping their futures."[7] In 1995, selections of this "agency model" research were published in a two-part special issue of the *Journal of Urban History*, "Toward a New African American Urban History." The edited book that followed was my introduction to this new way of writing about African Americans.[8]

While historians showed the way to write a historical or historicized geography of Tremé, this book is most clearly a product of the "geographic turn," the poststructural shift in thinking about space from sites where the social and political happened to constitutive of the human world we inhabit. Edward Soja refers to the interdependence of space and the social as the "socio spatial dialectic."[9] The linking of things social and spatial reasserts the importance of space, theoretically putting geography more than on par with history. In this case, *social* means much more than personal interaction or ways of living. *Social* also encompasses questions of identity, meaning that places have come to figure more centrally in understanding how people think about themselves. Place and spatial practices are now seen as essential in understanding how marginalized communities resist oppression. The importance of space/place is evident in both historical and contemporary research. Within Goings and Mohl's *New African American Urban History*, for example, the first three substantive chapters address the way African Americans resisted their oppression and celebrated their culture through explicitly spatial means such as parades and celebrations.[10]

Links have also been drawn among contemporary urban black communities, territory, and identity. Castells suggests that inner-city residents have countered their peripheral and exploited existence with "the defense of their identity, the preservation of their culture, the search for their roots, and the marking out their newly acquired territory." Foreshadowing the post-Katrina looting in New Orleans, Castells continues, "Sometimes they display their rage, and attempt to devastate the institutions that they believe devastate their daily lives."[11] Even though the work of theorists such as Castells, coupled with an increase in the production of urban ethnographies, has strengthened the link between ghetto and identity, some of these communities were already being dismantled by gentrification. This process, which Stephen Haymes terms "deterritorialization," has continued and accelerated, particularly after local governments became interested in the redevelopment of downtown neighborhoods and public spaces.[12]

Finally, while both the agency model of writing about black communities and political economic analyses of contemporary urban development are sufficient ways to conduct neighborhood-based studies, I also take cues from recent work in cultural geography, particularly the subfield of geography interested in cultural landscape. Cultural landscape studies have a long history in geography (and other fields) characterized by different definitions of landscape and differing methodological traditions.[13] Common within these different landscape traditions is the objective of interpreting landscapes to learn more about the societies that create them. Recent works look at the material or built landscape as both representative and constitutive of the various discourses that produce it. Of particular interest to this book is the work on race and landscape, which interrogates the ways that race, racial categories, racist practices, and/or racism make their way into the material landscape.[14]

This book is a contemporized historical geography of Faubourg Tremé. The story I tell is not one of a neighborhood where interesting things happened but one of a neighborhood that came to be through spatial processes — the spatialization of nation and race. The neighborhood has long been a place of marginalized people, who, through their daily lives and activities, have come to define it. But even as residents have continually tried to make their way in Tremé, others — most notably, people at various levels of government or groups of people with government assistance — have worked to alienate, dispossess, or deterritorialize those residents. I hope this volume does justice to those whose story has not been told in a sufficiently critical way.

ACKNOWLEDGMENTS

Writing this book has been a long journey that began here in Lexington Kentucky and took me to Louisiana, only to find me back in Lexington. Along the way, I was helped by more people than I can ever thank. Most important have been members of my family, who have been completely supportive of my academic career if not always sure what all it entailed outside of teaching.

The greatest thanks I have for this book go to my dissertation committee at Louisiana State University. Greg Veeck guided this project from start to finish. After reading the first draft of my proposal, he wrote to me, "If this isn't a book, I'll eat my hat." Dr. Veeck, you are off the hook. My committee also included Karen Till, Carville Earle, Joyce Jackson, Helen Regis, and Wayne Parent. Each of them not only contributed to the finished product but also shaped the kind of scholar I would eventually become. I am thankful to Karen for introducing me to critical human geography and to Helen, Wayne, and Joyce for their insights into the culture and politics of South Louisiana. I am also belatedly appreciative of the historical insights of Carville (and Anne Mosher). I am as much a historical geographer as anything else. The whole dissertation process was made bearable with the help of my fellow geography and anthropology graduate students. There are too many of you to name, but know that I cherish the times we spent together. I am also thankful for my friends in the Black Graduate and Professional Student Association for giving me a meaningful escape from geography and lasting friendships.

My fieldwork in New Orleans was greatly aided by my stint as a park ranger at New Orleans Jazz National Historical Park. It was during that time that I became familiar with traditional New Orleans Jazz and the cultural politics of Tremé. I am grateful to Gayle Hazelwood for the opportunity. I am also thankful to the people of New Orleans and Tremé who took the time to talk with me about my work and their lives. A special thanks to Jacques Morial for his insights into post-Katrina controversies in Tremé. I also need to say thank you and "You Next" to Papa Sunpie and the North Side Skull and Bone Gang. Masking with you on Mardi Gras Day for the past six years has been a special experience. I look forward to waking up Tremé with you in years to come. Fulfilling a promise, thanks to Jerry Roppolo; a lot of words have been written in your Rue de la Course coffee shops by me and others over the years. I also owe a debt of gratitude to Mary Barkley, Carlos Deloach, Ivan Guillory, Kim Chavis, Rosanne Adderley, and Mike and Ashley Ross for making their homes available to me. Without your hospitality, working in Louisiana would have been more difficult and expensive.

This book would be much poorer without the help I received from librarians and archivists from several libraries. I am most grateful for the assistance of Irene Wainwright and the staff of the Louisiana Division of the New Orleans Public Library and Bruce Raeburn and the staff at the Hogan Jazz Archive. I am also appreciative of the help I received at the Williams Research Center, Amistad Research Center, and Special Collections at the University of New Orleans.

I am also grateful to the University of Kentucky for awarding me a Lyman T. Johnson postdoctoral fellowship, which allowed a couple of years to plan the course from dissertation to book. Later the university's College of Arts and Sciences and Geography Department supported my frequent return research trips to New Orleans, many of which just happened to occur during Mardi Gras, but most during south Louisiana's oppressive summer months. During my time as assistant professor at the university I could have had no better cultural geography mentors than Rich Schein and Karl Raitz. Schein's work on landscape and race has been the greatest influence on my own work, and I am honored to have written a chapter in his volume on the subject. Without a semester-long set of hard deadlines and meetings with Karl, who introduced me to human geography over two decades ago, this book would never have made it off my desk. In my time at Kentucky I have also had the chance to collaborate on journal articles about New Orleans with my friends and colleagues Matthew Zook and Kathleen O'Reilly. Both papers gave me new lenses with which to examine Tremé and New Orleans.

Tate White, Wendy Gaudin, Judith Hunt, Maria Fontana, and Caroline Smith each lent their editing and organizational skills to my manuscript before its formal acceptance. Without your help, this book might never have been published. A big thanks to the University of Georgia Press for taking on this project when others didn't. Derek Krissoff, John Joerschke, and Ellen D. Goldlust-Gingrich have been incredibly patient with me. I think we have a good book though. I look forward to doing this again.

Tremé

Introduction

It was a dark day in New Orleans's Tremé neighborhood, perhaps the darkest since the Claiborne Avenue oak trees were felled nearly forty years earlier to make way for Interstate Highway 10. On 18 January 2004, "Papa" Joe Glasper, owner of a Tremé neighborhood bar, Joe's Cozy Corner, confronted street vendor Richard Gullette and demanded that Gullette stop selling beer outside Glasper's establishment and siphoning business away from the bar. After an initial confrontation that ended with Glasper accusing Gullette of physical assault, Glasper reentered his bar and then returned to the street armed with a .357 magnum handgun, with which he shot Gullette. The vendor would not survive the day. Gullette's murder was one of the first of 2004. By year's end, New Orleans had suffered 264 more.[1]

Tremé is not unfamiliar with gun violence. It is a low-income, predominantly African American neighborhood with all the negative indicators associated with similar places. Just like most neighborhoods, even rough ones, however, Tremé is full of caring, talented, hardworking people. Why, then, start this book with another example of seemingly senseless violence? The issues surrounding this case speak of far more than murder, both in Tremé and in inner-city neighborhoods across the United States.

The circumstances of Gullette's murder are morbidly fascinating because they involve layers of spatial irony and because they defy expectations. Moreover, the day's events and their consequences for the larger neighborhood simultaneously reveal both Tremé's storied history and its present cultural relevance. In a post-Katrina world where the Lower Ninth Ward has become as familiar a New Orleans neighborhood as the French Quarter, the Faubourg Tremé is culturally the most important and endangered of New Orleans's neighborhoods. To understand why, we must return to Joe's Cozy Corner.

The occasion that brought Gullette and Glasper together was the funeral—or, more appropriately, the events surrounding the funeral—of Anthony Lacen. Known across the city as Tuba Fats or simply Fats, the larger-than-life Lacen embodied New Orleans's African American performance traditions as did few others. He was arguably one the most influential tuba players in the city's history. The bands with which he played, including the Fairview Baptist Church Band, Olympia, Doc Paulin, Onward, Tuxedo, and Preservation Hall, are among the most storied in New Orleans's jazz and brass band history. Lacen was also present at two points when modern New Orleans music unquestionably changed course, if only slightly: the revival that resulted from the Fairview Baptist Church Band's formation under the guidance of the late jazz legend Danny Barke, and the transition that resulted in bands such as the Dirty Dozen and the current gold standard in New Orleans brass bands, the Rebirth.

Tuba Fats's most lasting contribution, however, may have been his role as a mentor to New Orleans's younger musicians, to whom he demonstrated both the possibilities and the pitfalls of the music business. All the while, Lacen played daily at Jackson Square, not necessarily for the tips but for the love of the music and the people. Upon his death, Tuba Fats received the posthumous honor to which every New Orleanian "in the tradition" — whether that tradition is music, masking, or parading — aspires: a jazz funeral.

The jazz funeral, along with the anniversary parade, is part of New Orleans's "second-line" parading tradition, a unique institution practiced primarily in the city's African American communities. For centuries, these parades have passed through New Orleans's African American neighborhoods, stopping on occasion to commemorate or honor important people and places. The parades are called second-line because they are characterized by the throngs of neighborhood residents, "second-liners," who follow behind the procession's first line, which is comprised of the brass band and the parade's sponsoring organization.[2] A few of the second-line clubs from Tremé include the Black Men of Labor, Dumaine Gang, and the Tremé SideWalk Steppers.

Both Gullette and Glasper were playing common if not well-defined roles in Tuba Fats's second-line funeral. Gullette was a vendor, one of up to several dozen who typically accompany such neighborhood parades as they wind through miles of New Orleans streets for as much as four hours at a time. The vendors sustain and refresh the second-liners before, during, and after the parades by following along with shopping carts and coolers filled with beer and water or by positioning barbecue-grill-equipped pickup trucks in strategic spots along the route. These vendors hawk drinks and foods such as pork chops and hot sausage sandwiches as well as more traditional grill fare. One might also find local favorites such as boiled turkey necks, yak-a-mein, and sweet potato pies. These vendors, the quintessential urban entrepreneurs of New Orleans's informal street economy, play an integral role in the city's parading culture.

As a bar owner, Glasper performed a similar function. Neighborhood bars are built-in aspects of New Orleans's second-line tradition, often serving as home bases for second-line clubs and as points of origin and destinations for parades. In addition, bars also serve as stops along the route where club members and second-liners take short breaks. Each club uses its own criteria in deciding which bars to designate as parade route stops. Sometimes the reason is as simple as the bar's location. Other times, the bar may have a stated relationship with a club or high status in a neighborhood. Being chosen as a stop can definitely boost a bar's business. Because of most neighborhood bars' relatively small size and the hundreds or sometimes thousands of second-liners following each parade, territorial conflicts between vendors and bar owners are rare. There is usually enough business for everyone. On the day of the Gullette shooting, however, territory became an issue, maybe because Glasper's bar was not a planned stop on the parade route. The parade was scheduled to disband at St. Louis Cemetery No. 1, with a repast to follow at the Tremé Community Center. According to one account, as Tuba Fats's body was "cut loose," the crowd proceeded to Joe's Cozy Corner.[3]

Accounts of the shooting pitted Glasper and Gullette against one another, and each party had his share of supporters. The larger story, however, was driven by Glasper and the identity he had forged as the proprietor of Joe's Cozy Corner. The bar was located on the corner of Robertson and Ursuline Streets. In his years as its owner, Glasper became known as a no-nonsense proprietor with little tolerance for drugs or violence. He also had a reputation for being both stern with and generous to neighborhood children. By shooting Gullette, Glasper not only broke the law but also violated the terms of behavior that he had rigidly set and enforced.

Joe's Cozy Corner had reached the rare status of a popular neighborhood bar where New Orleans's musical traditions could be experienced in their natural and historical context. That opportunity lured outsiders, including tourists, who sought the neighborhood's storied performance traditions. Music—jazz in particular—has unquestionable significance for the development of New Orleans's tourist industry. But jazz is conspicuously absent from New Orleans's modern tourist landscape. During jazz's early years, it was regarded as an object of scorn and a corrupting influence. By the 1940s, however, New Orleans changed its tune, proudly proclaiming the once-demonized art form a local treasure. When the city began using jazz to lure tourists, it chose "safe" cultural channels, such as staged performances and passively experienced museums and archives, instead of the neighborhoods where the music originated.

One of the outcomes of this strategy was that it circumscribed the tourist experience. As Connie Atkinson suggests, in New Orleans, "music is used to assist in marking spaces where revelry is permitted. Music serves as a signal that a space is open for occupation. Within the French Quarter, where the music stops, tourists hesitate to venture."[4] In the city's tourist areas, traditional New Orleans jazz and brass band music is not highly visible. For example, none of the tourist-oriented developments between the Ernest N. Morial Convention Center and the Moonwalk, a riverfront promenade in the vicinity of Jackson Square, represent the city's musical heritage. Jazz, for the most part, is encountered in a few places in the Quarter, in a few nightclubs, and from street musicians in Jackson Square and the French Market. Bourbon Street, for all its lore, offers little in the way of jazz. Tourists are more likely to encounter popular dance music, blues, Cajun, and zydeco music. As romantic as it may seem to encounter a band playing on a French Quarter street corner, the reality of New Orleans's musical history is that places have always been important, even when talking about parading.

At its musical height, Joe's featured a Sunday double bill of local trumpeter Kermit Ruffins and his group, the Bar-B-Que Swingers, followed by the Rebirth Brass Band. That lineup brought carloads of visitors into Tremé. Black entertainment venues have always attracted whites (and blacks) seeking authentic cultural expressions, and even though Joe's Cozy Corner was situated on the periphery of tourist locations, it was part of that tradition. Tremé bars that serve or have served that function in more recent times include Sweet Lorraine's, the Little People's Place, the Mother-in-Law Lounge, and the Candlelight. In other neighborhoods, such bars include the Maple Leaf, the Sportsman's Corner (and former Kemp's) in Central City and Vaughn's in the Bywater. These bars differ from bars such as Tipatina's and Snug Harbor, which cater to citywide audiences.[5]

The Cozy Corner's role as an everyday neighborhood meeting place, however, was more important than its status as a tourist outpost. At least outwardly, the bar represented the community values thought to have bypassed Tremé and many other African American communities.

At a time when drugs and violence were plaguing Tremé and hip-hop and contemporary R&B songs played from jukeboxes in neighborhood bars, Joe's Cozy Corner was a throwback. Glasper's jukebox featured local music, including songs recorded by people from the neighborhood. The bar was also a place where people, particularly the community's older men, some of whom no longer lived in the neighborhood, passed by or checked in on a daily basis. Joe's

Cozy Corner had truly become a local landmark. It was tied to the neighborhood's traditions, and it was part of the neighborhood's culture.

New Orleans has a long history of similar neighborhood bars, most of them now long gone. As one traveler described the city in the first years of the nineteenth century, "At the corners of almost all the cross streets of the city, and its suburbs, are to be seen nothing but taverns, which are open at all hours."[6] When the suburb of Tremé was created in the early nineteenth century, it adopted that tradition. Rock and Roll Hall of Fame drummer Earl Palmer rattled off the Tremé bars of his youth more than 125 years after the neighborhood's creation: "In Tremé they had bars on every corner. They had the Crystal Club on Dumaine and Robertson, the Keno on Dumaine and Claiborne, the Struggle Inn and the Gypsy Tea Room on St. Ann, Joe Provenzano on St. Peter and Villere, Toni Heisser's on St. Philip and Claiborne, the Orange Room on St. Ann and Galvez, the Orange Liquor Store on St. Philip and Claiborne, and Roland's on St. Ann and Derbigny."[7]

Benevolent society halls also functioned as neighborhood meeting places. More recently, clubs such as the Tremé Music Hall, the Candlelight, the Little People's Place, and the Cozy Corner's predecessor, Ruth's, have played that role in Tremé. In many ways, then, Glasper's bar had been a typical Tremé institution. Increasingly, however, it was becoming atypical, an outlier, an outpost of an entirely different type.

Over the past few decades, Tremé's demographics have changed. The neighborhood's abundance of historic architecture and its proximity to the French Quarter have drawn increasing numbers of historic renovators. Tremé has always been a neighborhood of shifting demographics. Settled by Creoles of all races, the neighborhood first saw an influx of Italians and "American blacks," followed by an exodus of whites. Tremé has never been totally black, but since the first half of the twentieth century, blackness has characterized the neighborhood. Typically, the most immediate outcomes of this neighborhood gentrification process are the displacement of long-term residents as a consequence of the conversion of rental properties to owner occupancy and/or an increase in rents in renovated areas.

Many of these new residents seek a neighborhood experience that is at odds with what has characterized Tremé for more than a century. Newer residents desire to limit what many consider nuisances — loud and late-night music from neighborhood bars, block parties, and unsanctioned parading. These goals are usually accomplished with the aid of coercive police activity or, in the case of bars, by raising legal challenges to their legitimacy. These issues had been playing out in Tremé since the 1990s, most notably involving a small bar on Barracks Street, the Little People's Place.

Two years before Gullette's murder, another man had been gunned down at the Cozy Corner, and some Tremé residents already considered the bar a nuisance. As could be expected, a movement to close the establishment gathered steam. The New Orleans Alcohol and Beverage Control Board revoked the Cozy Corner's liquor license in April 2004, and Mayor Ray Nagin issued a press release stating that bars showing a pattern of crime and violence would be closed. At the hearing where Glasper's license was revoked, many of those speaking against the bar were Gullette's relatives. The eventual closing of Joe's Cozy Corner, however, can be seen as a victory for those seeking to clean up Tremé.[8]

The example of Joe's Cozy Corner highlights many of the current issues that are important in Tremé, including the controversy over the place of Tremé's long-standing cultural traditions in a changing neighborhood and the antagonistic relationship between the long-term residents of Tremé and the local government, particularly law enforcement. This matter also speaks to the general importance of Tremé and of neighborhood institutions, including bars. In addition, even though it is a local case, the incident reflects issues that affect many urban communities across the country, such as increasing gentrification and the related change in inner-city demographics and a renewed deterritorialization of urban communities in line with urban renewal and the interstate highway program.

In part, this book establishes Tremé's significance in New Orleans's contemporary urban political and cultural economy. Moreover, the volume details how the Tremé neighborhood became significant. This historical geography of Tremé focuses on how the neighborhood evolved through an array of spatially selective processes, including exclusion and segregation and targeted destruction and displacement. Through those disruptive and deterritorializing practices and residents' efforts at resistance, Tremé has come to have local and national relevance.

Tremé is not a monolithic community. It is neither entirely black nor all poor. There are white folks and some who consider themselves Creole. Since Katrina, Hispanics have become more visible. Even within the racial and ethnic groups present, people have different incomes, politics, and religious beliefs. Some of the white renovators, for example, love the neighborhood's public culture — the music, the bars, and the parades. Some blacks look on those same activities with disdain. Trushna Parekh's research on gentrification in Tremé reveals many of these attitudes.[9] As a result, any discussion of "a Tremé community" or "black Tremé" is problematic, and this book employs the concept of community with that understanding. I consciously seek to distinguish among the communities being discussed and the issues, traditions, or places around which the community in question is formed. I focus on the Downtown, working-class African American neighborhood known as Tremé. (In New Orleans, "Downtown" refers to the section of the city below or downriver from Canal Street, historically the domain of the French-speaking population.) Within that neighborhood, I focus on the historical geographies of long-term residents and the institutions — public spaces, organizations, businesses, and traditions — that they have created or inherited to serve their community.

In chapter 1, I introduce Tremé. In terms of culture, political history, architecture, and community activism, few places in New Orleans are as important as this neighborhood. The French Quarter may be the city's showpiece and playground, but Tremé is its soul. Within the city's tourist economy, Tremé is viewed by many as the locus of the city's parading and musical traditions. Tremé is a paradox, however, because it is also one of the city's pariah neighborhoods. It has a predominantly low-income and black population and is bordered by two large public housing projects. Consequently, visitors are cautioned against venturing into Tremé. I begin by describing Tremé's exact location and explaining why the neighborhood's boundaries are important before turning to a discussion of how the neighborhood is represented as a place of culture and danger. I also include background on Tremé's history of radical Creole politics and the importance of music and parading.

Chapter 2 begins a spatial historical narrative of Tremé that looks at the social, economic, and cultural traditions that developed between the neighborhood's founding beyond the walls of the original city in the early eighteenth century and the first quarter of the twentieth century. Whether as the wilderness of the city commons or as a haven for Afro-Creole immigrants, the area has existed in opposition to the city proper, the American city, and finally white New Orleans. As an oppositional or counterspace community, Tremé developed a host of cultural institutions and traditions manifest in its cultural landscape.

In the first half of the twentieth century, crowded and dilapidated cities throughout the United States fell under the development ideology of the Garden City and City Beautiful movements. Those concepts, along with public housing initiatives, led to the clearance of areas deemed substandard. New Orleans was no exception. Chapter 3 looks at the processes of urban development in New Orleans, devoting particular attention to the places in Tremé that fell victim to those movements. Specifically, the chapter focuses on the city's efforts to create a civic center and cultural center in Tremé, employing the tactics of slum clearance and later urban renewal.

In terms of social and economic functions, no place may have been more important to Tremé than North Claiborne Avenue. The street's tree-lined neutral ground (median) provided space for everyday interaction and annual festive occasions, such as Mardi Gras. The street also served as New Orleans's Downtown black business district. Pharmacies, insurance companies, and grocery stores are just a few of the businesses that could be found on Claiborne. In the 1960s, the federal interstate highway program brought an elevated interstate down Claiborne Avenue, destroying the neutral ground and business district. In addition to discussing the importance of Claiborne and the details of its demise, chapter 4 asks the tough question of whether the interstate simply hastened the inevitable demise of Claiborne after integration.

The city's decision to create Louis Armstrong Park sprung from a desire to commemorate the legendary trumpeter's life after his 1971 death. The park also provided an opportunity to right the failure of the civic center and cultural center projects in the cleared Tremé area. Chapter 5 opens by exploring the issues of the first phase of the construction of Armstrong Park, including design and funding concerns. Particular attention is given to the conflict between the city's concertgoers and those interested in educational uses for the park. The chapter then turns to the second phase of the park's development, highlighting the Tremé community's attempts to fight privatization efforts and become involved in decisions about the park.

After the destruction inflicted by the urban renewal and interstate highway programs, the federal government returned to Tremé in the 1990s in the form of the National Park Service (NPS). With the NPS came the promise of federally funded and culturally based development. Chapter 6 relates the story of the New Orleans Jazz National Historical Park's creation in the context of the rise of the symbolic economy and heritage tourism. Again, the local community's efforts to become involved in the process of park development are discussed. In addition, this chapter chronicles the NPS's twenty-five-year effort to focus more on urban areas and social and cultural resources.

Chapter 7 speculates on the future of Tremé and its cultural traditions in an era of increasing gentrification. The neighborhood's middle-class gentrifiers often frown on the public music and parading traditions, and this chapter contrasts the efforts of Adolph Bynum, a black man transforming Tremé's dilapidated landscape, house by house, with the efforts of the long-standing community to maintain its way of life. This chapter emphasizes the changing nature of gentrification from a process defined by white outsiders to one involving affluent and knowledgeable African Americans.

Hurricane Katrina changed New Orleans more than any single event in the city's history save perhaps the U.S. purchase of Louisiana. The epilogue reflects on the ways in which changes inspired by Katrina have affected and will continue to affect Faubourg Tremé and particularly its long-term, working-class residents. The discussion includes several incidents that took place in the neighborhood following the storm, including the temporary closing of St. Augustine Catholic Church and, most importantly, the razing of the Lafitte housing project.

CHAPTER ONE

Creating Black Tremé

It's all like a web that had to anchor itself in various
aspects in the community.
—*Norman Smith*

Stepping out of New Orleans's lower French Quarter, one crosses Rampart
Street and enters the Faubourg Tremé.[1] The quick crossing into Faubourg Tremé
may be thought of as simply leaving one neighborhood for another — tourist
for residential, affluent for poor, white for black, safe for dangerous, dangerous
for deadly. In fact, one crosses several boundaries and enters many landscapes.
At first glance, the spectacle of Tremé differs not so greatly from that of the
French Quarter. With the exception of those along Governor Nicholls Street,
one of the city's oldest, trees in Tremé are small and sparse. As a general rule,
houses in both the French Quarter and Tremé appear to be small, with narrow
street frontage, and sit adjacent to the banquette (sidewalk), with little or no
front yard. Often, however, the houses are situated on deep lots and thus are
much bigger structures than appears to be the case when viewing them from
the street.

The architectural styles in Tremé are dominated by variants of the shotgun
house — single, double, and camelback — and so appear the same as the rear
residential section of the French Quarter. A few Creole-style cottages also exist.
In the first blocks across Rampart Street, the houses in the Faubourg Tremé are
in good condition; many have recently been renovated and painted in either
strikingly vivid or muted pastel colors. The social and economic characteristics
of this section of Tremé vary, but residents are whiter and wealthier than those
farther "Back o' Town" (that is, farther from the river). The houses deeper into
Tremé appear less well maintained; many are dilapidated, and some are burned
out. Vacant lots become more prevalent, as do houses and buildings that vary
from the traditional New Orleans architectural styles. The built landscape is
dotted with corner stores, bars, and occasionally more monumental churches

and schools. This section of Tremé is populated mostly by low-income African Americans whose lives are affected by the same social conditions that persist in similar urban communities across the United States: low educational attainment, low-wage occupations, unemployment, violent crime, and drugs. A large part of this landscape is consumed by Louis Armstrong Park, a thirty-acre public space fronting Rampart Street. The park contains an accidentally postmodern assemblage of monumental edifices, historic spaces, and buildings. The most important component is Congo Square, a nineteenth-century slave and Indian marketplace where African religious and musical customs were practiced during slaves' free time. Other noted structures include the Morris F. X. Jeff Municipal Auditorium, the Mahalia Jackson Theater for the Performing Arts, the Perseverance Hall Masonic Lodge No. 4, and the Rabassa and Reiman houses. Inside the fenced and gated park, these structures are variously arranged around landscaped berms and a cement lagoon.

Locationally and functionally, Rampart Street and Armstrong Park are the opposite of the French Quarter's Decatur Street and Jackson Square. Decatur is the city's main street for tourists. During the day, it is busy with visitors seeking French Market T-shirts, beignets from the Café du Monde, Central Grocery muffulettas, or photos of St. Louis Cathedral taken from the Mississippi River levee.

Situated between the river and the cathedral on Decatur Street is Jackson Square, which originally served as New Orleans's military parade ground. The square is now an immaculately manicured park, surrounded on all sides by a tall iron fence. At the square's center stands a statue of Andrew Jackson, commemorating his role in the Battle of New Orleans. Immediately outside the square's fence are art vendors, tarot card readers, and musicians, part of an ongoing debate about who should have access to the space. There is no public debate about activities and behaviors within Jackson Square proper, which are as closely regulated as the foliage.

This vibrant Decatur Street atmosphere has not always existed. Both its upper and lower reaches have seedy pasts, though both areas are presently stable. Lower Decatur is the home of bohemian and working-class bars and antique shops, while the House of Blues and Louisiana Music Factory anchor the blocks approaching Canal Street. The health of Decatur Street is neither an accident of location nor solely a product of entrepreneurial spirit. For many decades beginning with the New Deal, a concerted effort has sought to assure the viability of the larger riverfront area. In 1936, the French Market was rehabilitated under the direction and financing of several entities, including the Orleans Levee Board and the Public Works Administration. In the 1970s and 1980s, the construction of the Moonwalk, Woldenberg Park, and the Aquarium of the Americas, in addition to the demolition of deteriorating port- and wharf-related structures, improved the economic potential and aesthetics of the riverfront. Areas to the rear of the French Quarter have not received the same attention, however.

Running parallel to Decatur Street, six blocks to the rear, is Rampart Street. It has little of Decatur's charm and even less of its tourist activity. Functionally, Rampart Street provides a route between Uptown and Downtown for those wanting to avoid Interstate 10 or the Quarter's traffic. A 1940s ordinance removed Rampart Street from the architectural protections overlaying the majority of the Quarter; the street consequently is marked by vacant lots and parking lots and garages. The Vieux Carré Commission eventually reclaimed Rampart Street, but not before it fell out of the French Quarter's "tout ensemble." The street still contains many examples of the city's nineteenth-century architecture. A few structures are residential; most are retail. On the whole, Rampart Street remains peripheral to the vibrancy of the French Quarter.[2]

Across Rampart, Louis Armstrong Park has almost no pedestrian traffic. Since Hurricane Katrina, the park's gates remain locked except for special events, but even before the storm, little activity took place there with the exception of the ministrations of the grounds crew, the doings of a handful of transients, and visits from occasional walking tour groups having made their way from the nearby historic St. Louis cemeteries. Although the park's plants are well cared for, other markers of neglect can be found throughout. Benches are in disrepair, asphalt walkways lie crumbling, and litter lines the edges of the lagoon. The lagoon's bridges are in generally shabby condition and are missing their protective latticework. Throughout the park, paint is faded and peeling. The arched St. Ann Street entrance hints at the park's more festive past, even though many of the entrance's lightbulbs are broken.

Anyone familiar with urban morphologies cannot help but notice that the park is somewhat out of place amid the surrounding nineteenth-century neighborhoods. Indeed, Armstrong Park is the result of a series of failures between 1930 and 1970 to build civic and cultural center projects with easy access to Downtown.[3] As part of the process, the City of New Orleans demolished ten "deteriorating" blocks of the Tremé neighborhood. The project displaced scores of Tremé residents from their homes, making the neighborhood one of countless working-class African American communities across the country to fall victim to twentieth-century urban renewal projects.

In fact, these urban renewal projects can be seen as only one iteration of Greater New Orleans's attitude toward Tremé, an attitude that has repeatedly disrupted the community's stability. In the 1960s, for example, the Federal Highway Administration, with assistance from the state and local governments, routed Interstate 10 through Tremé. Like urban renewal, the interstate highway program commonly disrupted African American communities.[4] Although New Orleans suffered less residential displacement from interstate routing than did other U.S. cities, the project sped the destruction of the North Claiborne Avenue business district, which had catered to Downtown blacks excluded from shopping in segregated Canal Street establishments. The interstate also eliminated the oak-tree-lined neutral ground that provided leisure space for the community, particularly on Mardi Gras, when Downtown African Americans gathered to celebrate. The former neutral ground, now a linear parking lot running underneath the elevated expressway, still attracts people on Mardi Gras. On a daily basis, however, Claiborne Avenue's few businesses would hardly qualify as a district. Beyond Claiborne Avenue, Tremé continues to Broad Street.

Defining neighborhood boundaries is always a difficult project. The territorial limits of a neighborhood can be important because boundaries help determine both control of and access to resources. Boundaries may be drawn with reference to architecture, cultural traditions, or history. They matter to people, as neighborhoods can be a basis for identity formation. Even though boundaries depend somewhat on the people queried or documents consulted, a consensus exists that Tremé at least comprises an area bounded by Rampart Street, Orleans Avenue, Claiborne Avenue, and Esplanade Avenue, and the neighborhood may also extend upriver to Canal Street and lakeward to Broad. In between, there is room for discussion, including the contentious inclusion of the triangular section bounded by Claiborne, Esplanade, and St. Bernard. St. Bernard Avenue is roughly the boundary that separates Faubourg Tremé from its sister neighborhood, Faubourg New Marigny. This triangular section and its continuation across Claiborne are often not considered part of Tremé because the area lies north of Esplanade Avenue, in the Seventh Ward.

Determining Tremé's territorial extent is complicated by New Orleans's ward system. Wards are long-standing political districts formerly used for local and state elections and presently used as a basis for property assessment.[5] The stability and longevity of New Orleans's ward boundaries have fostered an association between geography and social, economic, and political status.[6] For example, the Fifteenth Ward has long been associated with the west bank community of Algiers, the Seventh Ward with Creoles, and the Third Ward with politics. Presently, the Ninth Ward is associated with the devastation of Katrina. According to the Bureau of Governmental Research, ward identity "was quite prevalent in the prior history of the city. Part of it is historic, part is neighborhood association. However, with the advent of rapid transportation and a high degree of population mobility, it is rapidly dying out. At the present time it exists probably among older population groups, those associated with politics, and in certain neighborhood ethnic groups."[7] At the time of its writing in 1961, there was likely no truer statement about New Orleans's wards. Older residents identified with wards because for decades wards were the basis for local elections, and ward-based civic leagues and improvement associations permitted residents to petition the local government for better services. Beginning in the late 1960s and 1970s, many New Orleanians began to identify with certain areas through other designations, like faubourg names. This switch was rooted in the loss of importance of wards in terms of politics and the rise in importance of neighborhood associations.

For many African Americans in New Orleans, ward (and housing project) association never waned. In recent years, however, ward-based identity has increased for younger residents based on the international success of New Orleans hip-hop artists. In the 1990s, several rap artists from the Uptown–Central City area became famous. The first rappers to have success were the artists from the No Limit record label, followed by musicians from Cash Money Records. The labels are loosely associated with the Calliope (B. W. Cooper) and Magnolia (C. J. Peete) housing projects, respectively. Residents of both projects and the general Central City area claim to hail from the Third Ward.[8]

Ward-based identity is thus imprecise: the Magnolia, Melpomene, and Calliope are not located in the Third Ward. The phenomenon can likely be explained by the fact that many of the area's residents are descended from people who were relocated from the actual Third Ward when part of that area was razed to build the city's current government complex.

Confusion about where one ward begins and another ward ends is also common in Tremé, where residents strongly identify with the Sixth Ward. The Sixth Ward technically begins at the Mississippi River and runs to Bayou St. John, with Esplanade Avenue and St. Philip Street serving as boundaries. The Neighborhood Story Project, an innovative exercise wherein residents of New Orleans's neighborhoods conduct interviews and write books about their neighborhoods, provides examples of both the importance and geographical imprecision of ward-based identity. Ashley Nelson's volume, *The Combination*, describes life in and around the Lafitte housing project on Orleans Avenue. The Lafitte is in the Fifth Ward, but its residents strongly identify with the Sixth Ward. Ebony Bolding's volume, *Before and after N. Dorgenois*, also features an expanded notion of the Sixth Ward. In this view, Faubourg Tremé is a separate part of the Sixth Ward located across North Claiborne.[9] In fact, many people commonly claim that until the 1960s, Tremé was known exclusively as the Sixth Ward. So when did Tremé become Tremé?

Given this complex mix of politics, culture, history, and identity, how can Tremé's boundaries be conclusively decided? The neighborhood's only undisputed boundary is Rampart Street. Other than that, no consensus exists. In short, neighborhoods are neither wholly compatible nor wholly incompatible with ward designations. Both political boundaries and historical settlement are valid neighborhood descriptors. But even though neighborhoods are complex, Tremé can be conceived as an area between Rampart and Claiborne that contains a concentration of structures, places, and social relations that are distinct and identifiable over time and in place.

This concern with wards and Tremé's territorial extent is not intended simply to confine or define the parameters of this book. In some ways, the neighborhoods beyond the ramparts of the original city have so much in common that certain distinctions are pointless. Nevertheless, neighborhoods have identities, and those identities have been formulated over time by processes that involve power relations and result in confrontations, inequities, and exclusions.

Beyond location and appearances, the neighborhood's significance is tied to what the area means in Greater New Orleans — or more important, what meanings people have attached to the neighborhood both inside and outside its boundaries, however ill-defined. Through lived experiences, hearsay, and media representations, Tremé has accrued certain meanings and associations. In short, the neighborhood has a public identity — or, more accurately, several public identities. Confirmation of the neighborhood's multiple identities is easily found by sampling descriptions of Tremé offered by various New Orleans organizations and agencies.

According to New Orleans's official tourist agency, "The Faubourg Tremé or as it is more frequently referred to, Tremé, is not only America's oldest black neighborhood but was the site of significant economic, cultural, political, social and legal events that have literally shaped the course of events in Black America for the past two centuries. Yet, few outside of New Orleans except for scholars and historians know its enormous importance to Americans of African descent."[10] The city's most powerful and prominent historic preservation organization, the Preservation Resource Center, describes the neighborhood as retaining "the feel of an old Creole New Orleans neighborhood. Second line parades and jazz funerals are still common, while several neighborhood bars are gathering places for musicians. Its architectural integrity and African-American heritage has [sic] drawn new residents from all over the country. At the same time, many Tremé families proudly trace their heritage in the neighborhood back four and five generations. Many old-timers can remember the days when musicians informally jammed on neighborhood stoops or around the wood-sheds in the evenings."[11] The neighborhood has at least three dominant positive identities: as a place of unique African American cultural performance tradi-tions; as a place of significant African American political achievement; and as a place of historic architecture. These identities are not mutually exclusive, and the first is the most dominant. Tremé is a neighborhood of colorful parades and funerals. It is a neighborhood where the city's carnival spirit is on display year-round. Moreover, it is a place where people can participate in the culture without knowing how to play an instrument or without belonging to a club. It is a place of second-line parades, DJs, jazz music and jazz funerals, corner bars, and black Mardi Gras and of all the foods and festivities that come with it.

Many times—in fact, at any time—Tremé may be the setting for second-line parades. There are as many definitions of a second-line parade as there are people involved in the experience, making any attempt at explanation all the more difficult. Unlike the Main Street parade, which has come to represent the typical parading experience in the United States, a second line winds through the streets of residential neighborhoods and particularly of black neighbor-hoods. Also unlike the typical parade, there is no separation between the pa-rade and the audience. The audience is part of the parade, moving along with it as people dance to the music of the brass band. A brass band and second-liners are the only requirements for a parade. Almost without exception, however, second-line parades are sponsored by neighborhood organizations known as social aid or social and pleasure clubs. Descendants of late nineteenth-century and early twentieth-century mutual aid and benevolent societies, these clubs have a continuing charitable and benevolent function but are most visible to outsiders when conducting anniversary parades or funeral parades (jazz funerals).

Tremé has a long history of second-line parades as a consequence of nu-merous benevolent societies. The neighborhood is still known for parading, serving as the home of the Tremé Sidewalk Steppers, the Dumaine Gang, and the Black Men of Labor, among other groups. On Sunday afternoons through-out the fall and spring, these groups celebrate their anniversaries with parades through the neighborhood. Tremé is also a neighborhood where jazz funerals have a long history and are still performed, again because of the presence of benevolent societies. The last of Tremé's parading traditions is that of the Mardi Gras Indian. Although of uncertain origins, the tradition is ostensibly a tribute to the relationship that African Americans and Native Americans developed as oppressed peoples during the city's colonial and early American periods.[12]

On Mardi Gras, neighborhood-based gangs, or "tribes," rove through black neighborhoods masked as Indians in search of rival gangs. In the event of a meeting, the tribes engage in ritualized combat, with the leaders, the "big chiefs," eventually coming face to face to engage in a battle of verbal toasts and to compare who has created the more beautiful suit. Each tribe spends the entire year constructing intricate suits of beads and feathers costing as much as several thousand dollars. Tremé's association with the tradition also comes from the long-standing practice of having most tribes travel to the Claiborne neutral ground.

All three traditions are colorful, vibrant, musical, and rhythmic. In varying degrees, all can involve spectators through call and response. Each of these traditions is rooted in and produces a unique cultural landscape. Bars, churches, cemeteries, streets, funeral homes, and neighborhoods are places where these traditions lend and derive meaning. According to Tremé resident Norman Smith, his neighborhood's unique culture is "like a web that had to anchor itself in various aspects in the community."[13] Smith is speaking specifically about the ways in which benevolent society halls were sites of political activism and the ways in which the halls and the neighborhood's funeral homes nurtured musical traditions. Cultural nodes (anchors, even) are connected by a street network and energized and given meaning by the ephemeral parade.

Tremé is also noted for the radical political activism carried out by its Creole of color residents in the nineteenth century. To many observers, the word *Creoles* and the phrase *Creoles of color* call to mind the exotic mulatto women born from the eighteenth- and nineteenth-century relationships between African women and white men euphemistically termed *plaçage*. Creoles also call to mind the act of racial passing, the act of situational or permanently living as a white person to gain the social or economic benefits of whiteness.[14] Most Creoles of color were free (hence the term *free people of color*), and many made important contributions to New Orleans as artists, scholars, politicians, craftsmen, and soldiers. Both their art and their activism were geared toward gaining full rights of citizenship for Creoles. During the Civil War and Reconstruction, Creoles from Tremé led the call for all freed people. To give voice to their concerns, Creoles started several radical newspapers. Tremé area Creoles' last concerted civil rights effort came with the organization of the Comité des Citoyens (Citizens Committee), which is most noted for its sponsorship of the landmark segregation case *Plessy v. Ferguson* (1896).

Tremé's identity as an architecturally significant neighborhood has solidi-fied since the early 1990s. Because Tremé was one of the city's first suburbs, the age of its structures has never been in doubt. However, acquiring historical status requires not only old buildings but also the political process — involving residents, local governments, and nongovernmental organizations — of decid-ing which architectural sites and neighborhoods are valuable and worth sav-ing. For most of the history of the preservation movement, Tremé has been deemed expendable. In fact, while the French Quarter was receiving protec-tions in the 1930s, planners were dismissing parts of the architecturally simi-lar Tremé as "deteriorating." Forty years later, when Faubourg Marigny's gen-trifying residents were establishing their neighborhood's significance, Tremé was avoided as a consequence of its proximity to public housing projects. By the late 1980s and certainly 1990s, a favorable housing market and the lack of available housing options in other Downtown neighborhoods made Tremé a destination neighborhood for those looking to renovate or speculate. Since that time, parts of Tremé have been designated a historic district. It is also not uncommon for preservation groups to petition to save dilapidated structures in the neighborhood.

Tremé also has negative associations. It is continually disparaged as danger-ous and violent, leading to a perhaps externally imposed negative identity. The same tourist publications and Internet sites that tout the neighborhood warn tourists to avoid certain parts of the area at certain times of the day.[15] Although crime occurs in Tremé, as in many low-income African American neighbor-hoods, the ways in which the neighborhood and crime are associated should be discussed.

On a typical sweltering New Orleans summer day, after several hours of map reading in the Williams Research Center of the Historic New Orleans Collection, I found myself in a Decatur Street poster and print shop searching for replicas of the maps I had just perused. After several minutes, I overheard a conversation between a shop worker, who could have been an owner or man-ager, and a male customer. I paid little attention to the conversation until the customer inquired, "What would you consider the safe areas of the Quarter?" The shopkeeper advised the visitor not to venture far past Bourbon Street. Perceptions and representations of crime are important because they influence other behaviors, which, in turn, can be detrimental to those without the power to produce their own images.

During the 1960s and 1970s, Tremé's crime issues (or the perceptions of them) limited the area's redevelopment, a contrast to events in other Downtown neighborhoods. In subsequent decades, the question of how to address Tremé's development and crime issues periodically arose.[16] The answer came in the 1990s not from academic or policy studies but from a combination of lower crime, the availability of mortgage capital, the lack of redevelopment options in other areas, and a new interest in the neighborhood's history and culture.

With the 1994 election of Marc Morial as New Orleans's mayor, the city formally took an interest in Tremé, targeting the area for city-sponsored improvements and selecting it as the location for the New Orleans African American Museum. The neighborhood also became a local historic district. In short, a preservation ethos was formally supported in Tremé, helping to encourage historic renovations and gentrification.

The neighborhood's new residents raved about its diversity, culture, history, and proximity to the French Quarter. However, Tremé's newcomers have not always viewed the neighborhood's traditions in the same light as its long-term residents do. As a result, some of these new residents have sought to restrict or limit aspects of these traditions, seeming to misunderstand such customs. Though they may be enjoyable for both participants and spectators, these traditions do not exist simply to entertain. They also serve as the basis for community building and political resistance. As Stephen Nathan Haymes writes, "Within the black urban communities place making and therefore the production of public spaces is linked with day-to-day survival. But it is within the realm of day-to-day life, of daily survival, that black urban communities create public spaces that allow them to develop self-definition or social identities that are linked to a politics of resistance."[17] Over the past forty years, Tremé's long-term black community has chosen to fight for its culture. Only time will reveal how successful such efforts will be.

CHAPTER TWO

Afro-Creole Tremé

In 1809, the New Orleans newspaper *La Gazette* ran a short one-column-wide article announcing the arrival of a shipload of destitute Cuban immigrants to the port of New Orleans.[1] The article was little more than a nineteenth-century press release. It provided no context for the immigrants' arrival and in no way speculated on the impact on or future importance of the migrants to New Orleans. Today, the impetus for and ramifications of the migration are well known. In the 1790s, the free mulatto planter class in the colony of Saint-Domingue revolted; the colony's former slaves followed, creating an independent Haiti. The decadelong conflict led to substantial outmigration, spreading Haitians across the New World. Thousands moved to Cuba, whence they were summarily evicted after the French invasion of Spain in 1808. Roughly ten thousand Haitian Cubans eventually made their way to New Orleans.[2] The Haitian influx, evenly distributed among formerly enslaved Africans, free mulattoes, and white Creoles, quickly doubled New Orleans's population. Without this massive infusion of Haitian-Cuban peoples, New Orleans Creole culture might have wilted under the pressure of Americanization. There would have been little need, for example, for the development of New Orleans's Creole faubourgs beyond the ramparts of the original city. In particular, Faubourg Tremé was formally created after the influx. The culture and institutions of those immigrants, in combination with New Orleans's preexisting Francophone population, distinguished those early faubourgs.

This chapter examines the development of New Orleans's Afro-Creole cultural landscape outside the French Quarter during the nineteenth century. I summarize the academic research on Creole New Orleans, devoting particular attention to events in Faubourg Tremé. The work of other scholars, mainly historians, provides the background for this chapter, offering us a good understanding of the evolution of New Orleans's Creole culture.[3] With few exceptions, however, this work has little geographic specificity other than a secondary emphasis on the Downtown areas of New Orleans where most of the city's free people of color lived. This unintended slight has resulted in knowledge gaps. For example, while we know when important events happened and where, we have little understanding of why those events happened where they did. More important, these histories tell us little about why places have particular meanings and how they came to have those meanings other than as settings. This chapter explores how the Tremé neighborhood of the late twentieth and early twenty-first centuries, a place of unquestionable if conflicting importance, came to acquire meaning. The story of Tremé begins in the first decades of the nineteenth century, but understanding the Creole culture that came to define the neighborhood requires us to start at the city's founding ninety years earlier.

The French carved New Orleans out of the wilderness, one hundred miles north of the mouth of the Mississippi River, in 1718. The fortified city quickly became the French capital of the Americas. As with other colonial endeavors, New Orleans was an exercise in controlling foreign lands and people, an exercise that required abundant slave labor, a strong military, and strong will. The majority of colonial Louisiana's slaves arrived directly from Africa in a short period of time. Most of the arrivals belonged to the Bambara ethnic group, a Mande people who originated in the interior of the Senegambia region. According to Gwendolyn Midlo Hall, these factors greatly affected and even structured New Orleans's unique Creole culture.[4]

By the mid–eighteenth century, Africans enslaved in South Louisiana were coercively engaged in producing indigo, rice, and tobacco, outnumbering whites by a ratio of two to one.[5] Contrary to popular interpretations of slavery as a plantation-bound experience, in Louisiana and in New Orleans in particular, slaves demonstrated considerable mobility and autonomy. Ingersoll writes, "The great majority of slaves, free white people, and free blacks lived in the adjacent plantation regions. To the town center, white and black resorted frequently to enjoy the social life there, or to conduct affairs in one of the official institutions. Travel between plantation and town center was frequent because it was easy."[6] Furthermore, as a sparsely populated frontier settlement, Louisiana required the construction and maintenance of significant infrastructure and protection from local Indians; many of those duties fell to blacks, again leading to their increased mobility.

Louisiana slaves' autonomy also resulted from their masters' difficulty in providing for basic necessities. During the colony's early years, the harsh and foreign physical environment failed to produce enough food for self-sufficiency. On several occasions, colonists in New Orleans were forced to evacuate the settlement and live with the local Indian population.[7] Such ongoing problems forced planters to provide slaves with time off during which they could hire themselves out as well as tend their own garden plots. The practice of masters hiring out their slaves or slaves hiring themselves out was fairly common in both frontier and urban settings, where skilled labor was in demand. There was always a danger that slaves would either run away or amass enough money to buy their freedom, but owners often had no other viable option. In New Orleans, the practice was designed to release planters from the obligation of providing for their slaves. Moreover, because slaves produced their own food, a market was created where surplus could be sold. The Mississippi riverfront was New Orleans's primary eighteenth-century marketplace. By midcentury, however, a secondary market of slave merchants appeared in the rear of the city. Jerah Johnson suggests that this market started on Orleans Street, just outside the city's fortifications, in the 1740s or 1750s.[8]

For the colonial Louisiana slave master, providing basic necessities for slaves was not merely a matter of protecting an investment. A series of laws embodied in the Code Noir of 1724 dictated how people of African descent were to be treated. The code's most important articles pertaining to slaves were those respecting the slave family unit (Article 43), sanctioning slave holidays (Article 5), and regarding baptism (Article 2). As a result of the code and the colony's practical needs, slaves were indeed mobile and at times autonomous. The Catholic Church was central to the lives of many slaves as it played the role of educator and aid provider, in addition to administrator of baptisms and other sacraments and operator of open, if segregated, places of worship.[9]

Any examination of slave life in colonial New Orleans would be incomplete without a discussion of Native Americans. As the colony's first slaves, Indians were omnipresent, especially in New Orleans, where Indian women commonly worked. Unions between native women and African slaves became common because many more male Africans arrived than did female Africans. In addition, African slaves frequently ran away and joined local Indians in their villages or in maroon communities. The most noted example of the complexity of the situation was the Natchez Massacre (1729), in which members of the Natchez tribe, with the assistance of African slaves, massacred more than two hundred white settlers.[10] In short, the Africans proved valuable to both the French and the Indians, particularly the Chickasaws and Choctaws, in their struggles for dominance in South Louisiana. Not surprisingly, the French expended considerable effort devising ways to prevent Africans and Indians from allying.

Of the social factors that existed in colonial New Orleans, the most far-reaching was the intermingling of African slaves and whites. The tradition of mixed-race marriages and concubinage had long been practiced in the New World, and the blending of French and African peoples constituted a notable characteristic of New Orleans's social structure. Arnold Hirsch and Joseph Logsdon have pointed out that New Orleans's pattern of race relations is much like that found in other New World slave societies that possess three-tiered, multiracial social structures "typified by an intermediary or mixed race with a social value somewhere between Whites and Blacks."[11] The biracial offspring of these unions always inherited the bonded status of their mothers. These interracial unions may have initially begun because of demographics, but a system soon developed wherein white males selected African or mixed-race mistresses and entered into relationships with them. This relationship, called *plaçage*, often existed simultaneously with the man's formal marriage to a white woman. *Plaçage* relationships, also known as left-hand marriages, were carried out under certain guidelines.[12] Foremost, the man had to provide for both the woman and any offspring of the relationship. Such women and their children were often placed in small but comfortable houses. The relationships produced a class of people variously known as *gens de couleur libre*, free people of color (FPC), or Creoles of color. Members of this group often inherited property and money and reaped benefits derived from their partial whiteness.[13]

The French use of slaves and FPC as soldiers in defense against hostile natives proved the most significant colonial development for both slaves and FPC. Those initial experiments led the French to commission a standing black militia.[14] The Spanish expanded the practice, creating separate militias of light- and dark-skinned blacks. Military service could provide slaves with an important route to manumission. For those already free, military service had material as well as social benefits. Caryn Bell notes that the black militia offered "a major vehicle for free Black advancement and an esteemed social institution within the Black community."[15] The greatest value of military service, however, may have been symbolic. Service in the face of danger became a basis (along with general humanitarianism) for calls for equal treatment of blacks following the Louisiana Purchase.

Although New Orleans's FPC and slaves were governed by the same set of laws during the French and Spanish colonial periods, members of the two groups led very different lives, and their histories are often told separately. Some evidence, however, points to the interaction between these populations. For example, according to Hall, in the late 1790s, the government tried to ban dances sponsored by the free black militias because the number of slaves of both sexes often outnumbered the number of free persons.[16] The fact that

African slaves and free people of color socialized together during this period should come as no surprise. The eighteenth-century free population was fairly small, as was the city of New Orleans. Most important, even under a relatively liberal social system for the time, both groups were oppressed based on their Africanness. In the words of C. C. Robin, a naturalist who visited Louisiana at the beginning of the 1800s, "Thus, free or slave, black or mulatto, they seem to form a single family united in their abjection. They never approach each other without displaying signs of affection and interest, without asking each other news of their relations, their friends, or their acquaintances."[17] Though Robin specifically referred to the first years of the American period, such affinity existed not only throughout the French and Spanish periods but also through the nineteenth century.

TREMÉ

Although Claude Tremé did not begin subdividing his plantation until 1798, noteworthy activities were already taking place beyond the ramparts of the original city during the mid-eighteenth century. As Mary Christovich and Roulhac Toledano assert, "Faubourg Tremé is the history of the road to Bayou St. John."[18] The road, Bayou Road, began as an important high-ground portage running from the Mississippi to the bayou. Land on either side of the road was divided into plantations and successively subdivided until the area was formally incorporated into New Orleans in the early nineteenth century. The first and largest of those concessions went to engineer Charles Morand. Tremé came into possession of Morand's land in 1794 through marriage. Real estate transactions along Bayou Road attest to the presence of FPC as landholders.

While land along Bayou Road quickly changed hands, the area behind the upper part of city, known as the City Commons, remained largely undeveloped. According to Christovich and Toledano, "The inhabitants of the city were in constant habit of using all the land to the rear of the city according to their own use and doing other acts as suited their convenience and necessities."[19] In 1788, a cemetery was built behind the existing City Commons hospital; that cemetery eventually became known as St. Louis I. In 1792, construction began on Carondelet Canal for the dual purposes of draining the back swamp and providing a water route to Bayou St. John.[20] The canal's drainage function enabled the development of neighborhoods such as Tremé. The canal ultimately became a de facto border, separating Tremé's plantation from the City Commons.

The defining boundary of the colonial period, however, was not the canal but the walls that circumscribed the city limits. From New Orleans's founding, the city was surrounded by an unimproved military commons. In 1760, the French constructed fortifications around the city. Whereas the old military commons ran in a straight line along the rear of the city, the new fortifications extended outward into the City Commons. The fortifications apparently never conformed to their cartographic representations, however; the revised fortifications brought the slave marketplace, the Place des Nègres, within the city walls.

At the close of Louisiana's colonial period, a very intimate social geography existed within New Orleans's walls. The African-descended population, which by that time outnumbered whites, was relatively highly skilled and mobile compared to their Anglo-American counterparts. Because of their unique social status, African slaves and FPC carved out (or had designated by law) a few spaces of their own. The highly racialized society thus failed to produce an explicitly racialized landscape, at least as we presently understand it. Church services, for example, intensely segregated along racial lines in the contemporary American experience, were segregated only internally. Also, no strict or mandated residential patterns existed. We do know that any money a slave earned could contribute to the price of his or her freedom. Other important slave spaces may have existed, but we currently have no evidence regarding them.

Two social functions, the Quadroon Ball and the Bals Cordon Bleu, were directly linked to the FPC's marginal status. The better-known Quadroon Ball was designed to further the institution of *plaçage* by showcasing mixed-race women to white male suitors. Upon approval of the woman's mother, the woman and her suitor could enter into a *plaçage*. Cordon Bleu was the name given to the most respected FPC families. At Bals Cordon Bleu, also known as society balls, admittance required an invitation, whereas admission to Quadroon Balls was governed only by the ability to purchase a ticket. The Bals Cordon Bleu were "designed to facilitate [the] survival [of people of color] as a race."[21] Society balls thus highlight the elitism long associated with Creoles of color, which gave birth to a color fetishism that has divided the city's African-descended population for more than two centuries.[22] Outside observers have widely condemned *plaçage* as little more than high-class prostitution. Scholars of FPC, however, are quick to defend the practice as a complex survival technique that existed because of the legal vulnerability of FPC women and the dearth of FPC men.[23]

AMERICANIZATION

In 1803, the United States purchased France's Louisiana Territory. The process involved much more than a simple switch in colonial administrations. The territorial exchanges between France and Spain in 1762 and 1800 appeared in many ways seamless because the population remained overwhelmingly French. The Louisiana Purchase, however, brought together two distinctly different populations. Americans arrived from the north with differing linguistic, legal, and religious traditions. Unlike the Spanish, the Americans were intent on imposing their ideas of social order on Louisiana. These changes posed a very real threat to the Creole ways of life and led to an antagonistic relationship between the two peoples. One rumored outcome of Creole and American antagonism was a prejudice that compelled the newly arriving Americans to reside as a group upriver from Canal Street in the Faubourg St. Marie, creating two culturally distinct areas.[24] Although the boundary between the two sectors of town was nowhere as absolute as is portrayed in New Orleans mythology, the resulting upriver/downriver (Uptown/Downtown) cultural division replaced the city walls as New Orleans's most significant boundary. The dialectical social tensions between Creoles and Americans shaped New Orleans's landscape, particularly Tremé.

These tensions played themselves out in several ways, the most notable being New Orleans's division into three semiautonomous municipalities during the period from 1836 to 1852.[25] Within the French population, slaves and FPC faced increasing restrictions throughout the nineteenth century, leading FPC to form separate institutions in an attempt to maintain their former privileged status.

Following the Louisiana Purchase, Creoles of color confronted Americans with demands for equal citizenship. Louisiana's governor and territorial assembly responded negatively. The territory's policy toward Louisiana's racial system was communicated in the declaration that "free people of color ought never insult or strike white people, nor presume to conceive themselves equal to whites."[26] Americans not only denied full citizenship to free people of color but also systematically and aggressively attacked what they perceived as a liberal social system that saw blacks freely roaming the streets and socializing and worshipping with whites. These attacks affected slaves and Creoles differently, but both formed institutions that fostered group identity and helped them cope with their increasing repression.

One of the first targets of increasing Americanization was the mobility and autonomy of slaves. For several decades, the Catholic Church in New Orleans continued its liberal stance toward blacks, but in areas outside of church influ-ence, repressive policies took hold immediately. Unlike FPC, slaves owned no property and had no legal standing. Therefore, they had no means to respond directly to the new repressive policies. One of the first policies affecting slaves was an 1808 police ordinance forbidding slave dancing "except on Sundays, at such places only as may be therefore appointed by the mayor, and no where else."[27] African slaves had danced in New Orleans and rural Louisiana since their importation, and restrictions on dancing logically sought to limit slave interaction that might lead to insurrection. It is likely that the Place de Nègres provided space for slave gatherings, and it eventually challenged the "Quadroon Balls as antebellum New Orleans's most celebrated public black institution."[28]

Following the Louisiana Purchase, Governor C. C. Claiborne ordered the dismantling of New Orleans's fortifications to encourage the city's growth. When the city incorporated the Tremé plantation and the City Commons in 1812, the area where Fort St. Ferdinand and the old slave market once stood remained an open space, designated Place Publique. There, the original slave market continued. Around the same time, the square became the setting of a seasonal attraction, the Congo Circus. The circus's regular appearance influ-enced people to refer to the square variously as Congo Plains, Circus Place, and eventually Congo Square. More important than its name were the weekly activities that occurred there.

The Sunday dance and music rituals were by-products of the square's mar-ket function.[29] Over several decades, however, the market functions dwindled, likely because of competition from other markets. The French Market had little effect on the slave market until 1823, when a centralized vegetable vending fa-cility was added. The slave market also suffered from the presence of boat ven-dors docked nearby at the Carondelet Canal's turning basin. The final blow to the slave market came with the opening of the Tremé Market in 1839–40.[30]

As the market functions declined, police ordinances continued to concen-trate on slave gatherings. The 1808 ordinance, for example, was repeated in 1817.[31] With each restrictive ordinance, the square became increasingly associ-ated with music and dancing. Travelers who visited New Orleans following the Louisiana Purchase documented the cultural differences between Louisiana and Anglo-America, paying particular attention to the cultural activities of the city's black population. Much of what we know about the status and activities of slaves and FPC is drawn from the recorded observations of these travelers.

The most detailed account of Congo Square's activities comes from the writ-ings of Benjamin Latrobe, an engineer who visited New Orleans in 1819. One Sunday afternoon, Latrobe was exploring the rear of the city when he encountered what he estimated to be five or six hundred dancers at a public square.[32] Latrobe's account provides important information about the gathering, including the Africanness of the performances' language, dances, and instrumentation. Scholars have used the Africanness of Congo Square's performances to illustrate the significance of New Orleans in the development of African American music and dance traditions. Following the square's policing and development history also provides insights into the status afforded slaves in antebellum New Orleans. Most important, whether viewed as performance space or market area, Congo Square must be considered a place of active resistance to the dominant slave society.

CREOLE TREMÉ

By the time city officials began restricting slave gatherings to Congo Square, the subdivision and settlement of Faubourg Tremé was taking place. An 1803 New Orleans map shows the early subdivision of Tremé into lots. In 1807, a surveyor laid out Faubourg Marigny, making it New Orleans's first suburb. Two years later, Joseph Pilie plotted the adjacent Faubourg New Marigny. City surveyor Jacques Tanesse officially plotted "the New Faubourg Tremé" in 1812.[33]

From its earliest development, Faubourg Tremé was an integrated neighborhood. Real estate records indicate that free people of color were involved in many of the neighborhood's early transactions, and free colored women owned many of the properties.[34] While there is no evidence that free people of color were ever numerically dominant in Tremé or more prevalent in Tremé than in areas such as Faubourg Marigny or New Marigny, their accomplishments make their presence in Tremé noteworthy. Most of the city's prominent free colored soldiers, politicians, developers, and musicians lived in or were associated with the area. The institutions and organizations they created imbued the neighborhood with a politics of resistance fitting for a people whose status was so close to the promises of freedom. But their Africanness, however faint, posed a threat to the dominant racial order.

The American desire to repress New Orleans's FPC proved to be more difficult than limiting the liberties and mobility of slaves. Americans worked to limit the growth of the free colored population by restricting the immigration of foreign-born and nonnative FPC as well as tightening manumission laws. FPC received a brief reprieve when the government, fearing a slave revolt and a British invasion, commissioned black militia units in 1814. The slave revolt never materialized, but two battalions of FPC were raised to defend New Orleans against the English. Racially oppressive conditions returned in the

1830s, but black Creoles escaped many of the effects because of New Orleans's division into three municipalities. The new territorial arrangement provided Creoles some level of security, but the governing decisions of the time reveal a heavy-handed American cultural bias. FPC had already begun to organize themselves into social clubs, the first of which were the Société d'Economie (Economy Society) and the Société des Artesans (Society of Artisans), both founded in 1834. The Société d'Economie was organized by upper-class, professional Creoles of color and distinguished itself based on the members' elite characteristics. The society was based in Tremé and in 1857 constructed a monumental new hall at 1422 Ursuline Street. Economy Hall and St. Augustine Church subsequently became the neighborhood's most important buildings. The Société d'Economie's exclusiveness, possibly an outgrowth of the thinking that produced the Bals Cordon Bleu, provoked members of the colored working class — military veterans, artisans, and craftsmen — to form the Société des Artesans "for colored mechanics." The society's primary function was to provide a forum for radical romantic literature.[35] Despite their differing origins and orientations, both societies and other antebellum organizations reinforced the social structure in the Creole of color community.

The creation of the municipalities may have temporarily insulated FPC from creeping Americanization but was less effective at protecting the Catholic Church's liberal religious traditions. From the first decades of Americanization, New Orleans's religious leaders attempted to realign St. Louis Cathedral's liberal religious traditions with the conservatism of southern planter society. For more than forty years, the church's French-speaking board of trustees stonewalled the American bishop's attempts to install pastors sympathetic to American religious sentiments.[36] Integral to the trustees' governance of St. Louis Cathedral was their prominence as French Freemasons. The trustees' egalitarian Masonic ideals contributed to the "strong current of religious ecumenism at St. Louis Cathedral."[37] Following a protracted battle, however, the trustees lost control of the cathedral, dramatically changing the city's cultural landscape. The cathedral's new racial dynamics and their effect on FPC were mediated by the construction of St. Augustine's Church, however.

According to John Alberts, St. Augustine Church — founded in the city by Father Rousselon on property owned by free people of color and built with the resources of those free people of color and the assistance of the Holy Family Sisters — had a large congregation, nearly half of it black.[38] Technically Alberts is correct. From its founding, St. Augustine served Tremé's growing population of white Creoles, French immigrants, FPC, and slaves. St. Augustine was never designated a black parish, as some Catholic churches were in the 1890s. The context of St. Augustine's creation, however, explains why popular belief identifies St. Augustine as a black church.

The Catholic Church played a central role in shaping the system that governed the lives of Louisiana's slaves and FPC, including the design and enforcement of the Code Noir. The church's outreach activities demonstrated a commitment to the individual and community well-being of members of both groups. During the French colonial period, for example, Ursuline nuns educated both free and slave females of African descent. In the American period, the number of religious groups organized to provide aid to poor FPC and slaves increased following the influx of thousands of indigent Haitians from Cuba.[39] In the 1830s, Catholic FPC, in cooperation with Martha Fortier, created a school to educate free colored girls. Part of the girls' training included instructions for proselytizing slaves. In the 1830s, Marie Jeanne Aliquot, a French émigré, began overseeing Fortier's school. In 1834, Aliquot moved the school from the French Quarter to the Tremé plantation house, briefly the site of the College d'Orleans. There, a group of free colored women, including Fortier protégé Henriette Delille, organized themselves as Sisters of the Presentation. The school operated until 1840, when financial strain forced its sale. The Ursuline nuns purchased the school under the condition that it continue the education of colored children. In 1842, after a series of setbacks, the Sisters of the Presentation were formally recognized as the order of the Sisters of the Holy Family. The order continued to promote the goal of educating Tremé's poor African-descended population, running several schools and asylums.

St. Augustine's origins lie in the initiatives of New Orleans's free people of color, who petitioned Bishop Antoine Blanc for the church's construction. The site chosen was the corner of Bayou Road and St. Claude Avenue, adjacent to the Tremé plantation house. Aliquot is purported to have been a major catalyst in St. Augustine's creation. In 1834, fourteen FPC placed the church's capstone. During the months preceding the church's opening, FPC aggressively purchased pews, leading neighborhood whites to buy their own and initiating the War of the Pews. FPC also purchased pews specifically for use by slaves. St. Augustine was dedicated in October 1842. The congregation was wholly integrated. The following month, Henriette Delille and Julie Gaudin knelt at the St. Augustine altar, committing themselves to the care of indigent FPC.[40]

Even though the construction of St. Augustine represented a victory of sorts for the FPC and slaves residing Back o' Town, the American Catholic Church's racist and segregationist practices forced many FPC to find solace in what Joseph Logsdon and Caryn Cosse Bell call "traditional French anti-clerical" outlets, including Freemasonry, spiritualism, and romanticism.[41] All three provided FPC with opportunities to critique governments' increasingly hostile racist practices.

Fueled by the assimilation of Irish and German immigrants, New Orleans's American residents won the city's reunification in 1852, thereby ending the limited autonomy of the city's francophone-dominated sections. According to Joseph Tregle, by that time, Creole (French) New Orleans had fallen behind the Americans in almost every indicator except numbers. The Creole community was no longer able to pose an effective challenge to the wealthy, powerful, and rapidly increasing American population.[42] In addition, a fear of slave uprisings and the specter of the northern abolitionist movement led to increased violence against slaves and free blacks. Across the South, blacks experienced a similar escalation in racial hostilities.

The dominance of racist Americans forced FPC to abandon their intellectual and aristocratic pursuits to support themselves in trades. The weakening of privileges for FPC was an important factor in the furthering of Creole radicalism. The term *Creole radical* refers to a group of politically active, French-speaking Creoles of color imbued with the egalitarian republican principles of revolutionary France and the Caribbean. Throughout the nineteenth and twentieth centuries, the radicals rejected the oppression of the U.S. dual racial order, seeking the abolition of slavery and universal male suffrage based on the humanitarian documents of the French and American Revolutions. These Creoles abhorred the attitude of the minority of Creoles who attempted to pass for white or to use their distinctive history as a basis for privilege.

The connection between New Orleans's FPC, many of whom lived in Tremé, and the radical thinking of Masons, spiritualists, and romantic writers is understandable given their French ancestry and threatened social position. This connection was strengthened by the fact that many of the organizations to which Tremé residents belonged were headquartered in the neighborhood. Prior to the Louisiana Purchase, the Étoile Polaire (Polar Star), organized in 1796, met outside the city walls in what would become Faubourg Tremé. In the 1850s, the group constructed a lodge at 1433 North Rampart/St. Claude. What would become Perseverance Lodge No. 4 was organized in Haiti in 1806. The group followed the migrations of other Haitians to Cuba before arriving in New Orleans, where it built a hall at 901 St. Claude in 1820.

With the onset of the Civil War, radical Downtown Creoles made a concerted push for abolition and equality for FPC at both the local and national levels. Many of the prominent figures in that movement were Tremé residents. Paul Trevigne, for example, edited *L'Union* and *La Tribune*, newspapers that advocated radical Creole politics. The *Tribune* was the nation's first daily black

newspaper. Prominent Tremé resident François Boisidore also figured prominently in the movement as an orator. In addition, Economy Hall, once the refuge of aristocratic FPC, hosted abolitionist and Unionist speeches and debates
during the 1860s, and in 1863 a group of black militiamen organized a vigilance
committee that met there.[43] In the fall of 1864, radical white Unionist Thomas J.
Durant spoke to a black audience at Economy Hall about the virtues of the
Union cause.

Radicalism also found a home again in the Catholic Church. Father Claude
Pascal Maistre was suspended from his Bayou Road church, St. Rose de Lima,
for vocally advocating emancipation, abolition, and religious egalitarianism.
Though suspended, Maistre oversaw a schismatic parish at St. Rose until forced
out at the start of 1864. With the help of Creole Radicals Charles Dolliolle,
Charles Honore, and Armand Gonzales, Maistre constructed Holy Name of
Jesus in the heart of Tremé at Claiborne and Ursulines Streets.

Following the war, Economy Hall hosted balls to benefit the Freedman's Aid
Association and to support universal suffrage. Congo Square also was the site
of important events. Father Maistre's black congregation mourned President
Abraham Lincoln's assassination by marching to Congo Square, and on 11 June
1864, a group primarily composed of "colored citizens" gathered there for an
emancipation celebration.[44]

Despite the best efforts of radical Creoles, the gains brought by the Civil War
gradually withered away. Immediately following the end of Reconstruction,
Louisiana Democrats segregated public accommodations. Tremé Creoles' last
and best effort to challenge the normalization of white supremacy involved a
plan to challenge Louisiana's public accommodation law at the federal level.
In 1890, a group of radical Creoles organized themselves into the Comité des
Citoyens (Citizens' Committee) and devised a plan to have one of its members, Homer Plessy, arrested for sitting in the white section of a passenger
railcar. Following Plessy's arrest, the committee sued on the basis that the
separate-car law violated the Thirteenth and Fourteenth Amendments to the
U.S. Constitution. In 1896, the Supreme Court ruled against Plessy and his
supporters in the landmark *Plessy v. Ferguson* case, establishing the "separate-
but-equal" doctrine that paved the way for segregation in all aspects of
southern life.

For the typical New Orleans resident, regardless of race, life following the
Civil War was difficult. For FPC, now simply Creoles of color, disenfranchise-
ment continued. They shunned charity, instead turning inward toward mutual
aid and benevolent societies, which became increasingly common after the Civil
War. In addition, Emancipation created a class of freed people who filed into

New Orleans from the surrounding plantations. One of the biggest obstacles these men and women faced was maintaining their health, as was the case in other cities where people lived in crowded, unsanitary conditions. Joining one or more benevolent societies offered a means of assuring that health concerns were addressed. Through dues, fines, and taxes, benevolent societies provided or subsidized medical care and burial expenses for their members.

Four-fifths of New Orleans inhabitants belonged to some type of benevolent society. Between 1862 and 1880, New Orleans featured more than 220 prominent societies, among them "benevolent associations, militia companies, rowing clubs, Masonic, Odd Fellow, Eastern Star, Knights Templar lodges, religious societies, social and literary clubs, orphan aid associations, racial improvement societies, and baseball clubs."[45]

By the early twentieth century, New Orleans had nearly three hundred such groups. Although some clubs were socially heterogeneous, most were split along ethnic lines. Freedmen typically started local chapters of national organizations such as the Masons, Elks, and Eastern Star. Creoles, however, created organizations in the mold of the Société d'Economie, including the Jeunes Amis (Young Friends, founded in 1867) and the Concorde (1878), both of which were headquartered in Tremé. Several of these societies built meeting halls in the neighborhood.[46] These societies played a particularly important role in providing members with burial assistance, "paying for the bands to lead the processions, taking care of burial expenses, holding special rites over the body, marching in the special regalia in the funeral procession, and wearing mourning badges for the deceased."[47]

The growth in black societies of all types coincided with a rise in the popularity of brass bands, creating fertile ground for the development of one of New Orleans's most venerated traditions, the funeral with music. The marriage of parading and music in New Orleans's black community followed a logical progression. New Orleans's Afro-Creole communities began conducting funeral parades or processions no later than the early American period. By 1819, according to Latrobe, "the parade of funerals is still a thing which is peculiar to New Orleans alone among all American cities. I have twice met, accidentally, a funeral. They were both of colored people for the coffin was carried by men of that race, and none but negroes and quateroons followed it." Although both of the funerals Latrobe witnessed included priests and regalia, he does not mention the second-line structure or music.[48]

During the nineteenth century, parading was customary in many communities across the country, with military brass bands commonly participating. Black New Orleanians adopted this tradition, resulting in the New Orleans street band, a contributor to the formation of jazz and still a fixture in the city's parades. William Schaffer's *Brass Bands and New Orleans Jazz* is one of the few books that acknowledges the complex relationship between these two musical traditions.[49] Classically trained Creole of color musicians dominated New Orleans's post–Civil War musical scene. Their social demotion prior to the war forced professionals and skilled craftsmen to rely on their musical avocations for their livelihood. Fortunately, the city provided numerous opportunities for musicians to earn a living. In antebellum New Orleans, FPC musicians formed orchestras. With slight changes in instrumentation, dance orchestras could be converted to brass bands better suited for parades and outdoor picnics. Benevolent societies frequently employed both orchestras and bands.[50] By the second half of the nineteenth century, the brass band funeral, as presently practiced, became associated with black New Orleans culture.

Benevolent and social clubs frequently paraded, both to conduct funerals and to celebrate the anniversaries of the organizations' founding. In the early twentieth century, respected clarinetist George Lewis recalled, "We would play for parades every Sunday during the spring and summer. Each club would hold a parade on its anniversary every year. They still have one or two parades a week in New Orleans but nothing like what used to be. There are not enough musicians to play."[51] Another clarinetist, Edmond Hall, similarly remembered, "As for why New Orleans was such a musical city and had so many bands, I think one reason had to do with the clubs. There are a lot of private clubs and organizations in New Orleans. Two or three guys would get together, you know, and make up the club and it would grow. So, when a member of a club died, they would hire a band for his funeral, and if a club had a part in a parade, they would have a band for that too. All the clubs tried to outdo each other."[52]

These halls and lodges played important roles in the development and evolution of jazz. Tremé's two Masonic halls, Perseverance Lodge and Étoile Polaire, have only minor associations with jazz, but jazz musicians are believed to have played at dances and balls held at the two lodges.[53] Early jazz was also present at two other black benevolent halls, the San Jacinto and Equity.[54]

The Francs Amis Hall stood within a block of Tremé. Its designation as a hall of high importance to the evolution of jazz stems from its booking of high-society dance music as well as hot jazz.[55] A Creole hall, Francs Amis had an admissions policy that favored light-skinned Creoles.[56] According to drummer Warren "Baby" Dodds, when he and a Creole friend "got old enough, we used to go to Francs Amis Hall, but I couldn't get in until he would talk to those fellows at the door in Creole. Inside, the girls wouldn't dance with me until he'd tell them in Creole, 'Dance with him,' and would tell them I was from uptown and a nice boy."[57] Dodds's comments reaffirm the scholarly suggestion that the important distinction between blacks was cultural rather than racial. Creole violinist Paul Dominguez offers another perspective on the perceived differences between Creole and American blacks:

> You see, we Downtown people, we try to be intelligent. Everybody learn a trade, like my daddy was a cigar maker and so was I. . . . We try to bar jail. . . . Uptown, cross Canal yonder, they used to jail. . . . There's a vast difference here in this town. Uptown folks all ruffians, cut up in the face and live on the river. All they know is — get out on the levee and truck cotton — be longshoremen, screwmen. And me, I ain't never been on the river a day in my life. . . . See, us Downtown people, we didn't think so much of this rough uptown jazz until we couldn't make a living otherwise. . . . [T]hey made a fiddler out of a violinist — me, I'm talking about. A fiddler is *not* a violinist, but a violinist can be a fiddler. If I wanted to make a living, I had to be rowdy like the other group. I had to jazz it or rag it or any other damn thing. [Buddy] Bolden cause all that. He cause all these younger men Creoles, men like [Sidney] Bechet and [Freddy] Keppard to have different styles altogether from the old heads like [Luis] Tio and [Manuel] Perez. I don't know how they do it. But goddam, they'll do it. Can't tell you what's on the paper, but just play the hell out of it.[58]

Tremé's Economy Hall played a significant role in the development of jazz. George "Pops" Foster, a jazz musician who played in both Uptown and Downtown New Orleans, including Perseverance Hall, recalled that "Economy Hall was high class, compared to other halls like Hopes Hall. When you made the Economy it was like working Carnegie Hall."[59] New Orleans's most famous trombonist, Edward "Kid" Ory, also remembered playing at Economy Hall:

> The first job I got was at Globe Hall. It was a big place, had a capacity of about 2,000 but they tore it down later. Then I started working in Gretna [Louisiana] at weekends, and soon after at the Economy and Co-operators Hall. . . . I rented the Economy Hall and Co-operators Hall — I tied them up for a whole year — I rented both halls. I sometimes got Buddy Petit to work with me, and I'd put him at the other hall when I couldn't get anybody to play over there. Sometimes, I kept the Co-operators Hall dark, until I couldn't get any more in the Economy Hall, then I'd open both halls. . . . Louis [Armstrong] was with me when Pete Lala [a white Storyville proprietor] and I were running dances together at his place on Claiborne, between Conti and St. Louis Streets. Pete Lala got mad when I didn't cut him in on the dances at Economy Hall and the Co-operators Hall. So he got about fifty cops to go around and run my customers away. I felt I was going to

lose my health down there—I didn't like the climate—so I packed up and came to Los Angeles.[60]

All three of the halls Ory mentions were located in Tremé. They and many other neighborhood meeting halls had nonmusical functions as well. For example, many Downtown benevolent societies used Co-operators as their headquarters. Globe Hall likely hosted Quadroon Balls, and Economy Hall was associated with radical politics.[61] That Tremé had a host of benevolent organizations and multipurpose buildings did not make the neighborhood unique. In fact, both were common components of nineteenth- and early-twentieth-century communities. Tremé did, however, have a high concentration of spaces dedicated to civic organizations and a culture characterized by an inclination toward parading. In the daily lives of residents of Tremé and other Downtown New Orleans neighborhoods, social organizations and their associated halls were cultural and literal landmarks.

Nevertheless, the neighborhood of Tremé as it is presently imagined did not exist before the early twentieth century. Furthermore, there is no indication that residents of the area had a neighborhood identity distinct from that of Marigny or New Marigny. The area's dominant identity was Downtown. Some businesses used the Tremé name, which also appears on some maps, but as a place separate from the rest of Downtown and known for radical politics, a parading tradition, or a distinctive musical heritage, Tremé did not yet exist. By the time neighborhood identities developed within the larger Downtown area, ward designations began to supersede faubourg names, and the Seventh Ward became the most distinct Downtown neighborhood.

The author's first visit to Tremé, 1992.

The Armstrong Park entrance, 2001.

Perseverance Hall No. 4 Masonic
Lodge, 2000.

Postcard showing the completed New Orleans Municipal Auditorium, about 1950.

The design for New Orleans's cultural center, 1931. Courtesy of Louisiana Division/City Archives, New Orleans Public Library.

The Armstrong Park fence, 2001.

CHAPTER THREE

The Clearance for High Culture

In 1919, New Orleans's French Opera House burned to the ground. The Bourbon Street venue had recently emerged from several years of financial hardship brought on by World War I. The fire ended one of Creole New Orleans's most proud and long-standing institutions. From the late eighteenth century onward, New Orleanians of all classes had enjoyed the opera. Creoles of color, some of them classically trained musicians, professed a special affinity for the form.[1] In addition to its musical function, the opera was also a social institution reflecting the French community's liberal conventions. Given its social and cultural importance, the Opera House's demise marked the symbolic end of Old World French Creole public institutions in New Orleans. Creole culture — most notably, the French language — had been in steady decline since the 1850s.[2] The lifestyle of Downtown Creoles of color experienced the same decline as Creole culture generally but was magnified by the racialized implications of the *Plessy* decision. As a response, Creoles created new cultural institutions in the Downtown wards, including Catholic churches and schools, exclusive social clubs, and ward-based political organizations. Even those institutions, however, were becoming more American. For example, in the 1910s, the Société d'Economie, which had always recorded its meeting minutes in French, began recording them in English.[3] Around the same time, Creole of color Rodolphe Desdunes published *Our People and Our History* as a tribute to his people's artistic and political achievements during the preceding century.

The destruction of the French Opera House initiated a discussion among New Orleans's politicians and businessmen about the city's need for a large meeting hall to lure convention business. Such a facility would allow New Orleans to compete with other cities that were already hosting large meetings. In 1926, following several years of intense debate concerning the prospective facility's design, orientation, and funding, the city began moving toward the creation of a new auditorium. Instead of building the new auditorium on the French Opera House site, a commission chose a location to the rear of the French Quarter, in Faubourg Tremé.

The auditorium's construction ushered New Orleans into the era of mass tourism. From the outset, planners envisioned the facility as the centerpiece of a larger municipal complex.[4] For five decades following the auditorium's construction, the city cleared large swaths of residential Tremé to make the complex or its derivations become a reality. The process displaced thousands of Tremé residents, destroying its places of community, performance, and resistance. The dismantling of much of Tremé's built landscape and the deterritorialization of its residents succeeded because of policies that refused to acknowledge the neighborhood's poor and increasingly African American residents. Explicitly addressing the city's policy of creating public buildings and spaces within a larger urban context reveals New Orleans's ambivalent attitude regarding urban residential communities.

The auditorium's construction required the demolition of one square block of Tremé. Because relocation considerations for displaced residents were not a pressing concern in the first half of the twentieth century, little is known about what happened to those who had previously lived in the square. Documents indicate, however, that city leaders and the planners they hired believed the area to be deteriorating.

Harland Bartholomew and Associates, the firm the city retained to develop the plan in the late 1920s, included the auditorium as part of a larger public building group in its Comprehensive Planning Report. The report proposed a civic center with structures in the Vieux Carré and Tremé. City Planning and Zoning Commission chair Charles Favrot supported the suggested location because

1) It is apparent that the trend of commercial development is above Canal Street and moving back toward Claiborne Ave. No Civic Center should be immediately surrounded by intense commercial development.

2) This center is just six blocks from Canal St. which is a reasonable distance from the center of commercial activity.

3) The site is well surrounded with main arteries for traffic by which it can be approached with the least inconvenience and without passing through the traffic congestion of the highly developed commercial areas.

4) Property values throughout this section are low and will probably not materially enhance, so that its eventual acquisition will not be too costly.

5) The location proposed is on the same axis as the old Civic Center of the City of New Orleans, which has a very strong appeal for the formation of the new Center.[5]

Although the report introduced and expanded on the concept of grouping public buildings, its authors expressed no concern for the community, justifying its clearance because

> the property of this neighborhood is not valuable nor in a good state of repair. The neighborhood has shown little tendency to improve in recent years. It is believed that the creation of a public building group facing Beauregard Square and the Squares bounded by Rampart, Dauphine, St. Peter, and St. Ann would result in an appreciation of property values and in substantial improvements in the immediate vicinity. . . . The public building group plan would therefore stimulate and encourage a high character of building development in a district where it might otherwise not be expected.[6]

The planning documents and other accounts of the creation of the civic center offer little evidence that Tremé was deemed anything but a slum and no indication that residents' opinions were ever considered. Neither of these facts is particularly surprising. In the first quarter of the twentieth century, urban theorists expressed concern about the physical deterioration and overcrowding of cities, advocating several solutions to these problems.[7] These solutions generally involved incorporating nature into the city in the form of parks and green spaces or building virtue into the city with monumental architecture and civilizing public spaces. One of the most popular and less altruistic practices involved using transportation infrastructure and public building projects to eliminate slum areas. With its neoclassical architecture, the civic center design evoked elements of the City Beautiful movement, while the written comments suggest the city's desire to reduce its dilapidated housing inventory.

In addition to attracting the city's attention, Tremé's physical deterioration led to social and demographic changes in the neighborhood. In one of the few extant firsthand accounts by a white Creole of life in Tremé before it became a predominantly African American neighborhood, longtime resident Sidney Bezou recalled life "back o' town" as unique. According to Bezou, born in 1911, Tremé's physical decline culminated in an "exodus from the Esplanade Ridge." He attributed this outmigration to intermarriage between American men and Creole women. Following marriage to a Downtown Creole woman, Uptown men typically wished to remain Uptown, resulting in "an increasingly lower economy for the remaining Creoles." Moreover, after World War I, the community experienced a loss of homes on Rampart, the "mecca of society." Bezou thus insightfully connected the neighborhood's decline and New Orleans's policy of neglect: the city "did not have the foresight to improve the area where it would remain a sort of French Quarter which would have been an attractive section for the visitors, the tourist trade which was not very well given consideration in the time of WWI or thereafter. . . . But just the reverse took place. . . . It is here that I must consider the demise of the faubourg took place, and most of the Creoles, even those of less economic status, had to make one decision, to move away."[8]

Bezou's words do not mean that all whites, Creole or other, left Tremé at the same time. According to one white woman born during the Great Depression, her family did not move from a big house on Claiborne Avenue near Esplanade to the vicinity of Esplanade and Gayoso until 1951. She liked living around blacks in Tremé and remembered seeing black women walking with items balanced on their heads. Her church was one-fifth black, including half of the altar boys, as were half of the students at her school. During her childhood, the area's many whites gradually moved away. When her family left, they, like many others, sold their home to black people.[9]

CIVIC CENTER

New Orleans's Municipal Auditorium opened in 1929–30. Construction had required the destruction of Globe Hall, located on St. Claude and St. Louis Avenues. Globe Hall had arguably been one of the most important Downtown dance halls for blacks. Even prior to the auditorium's completion, however, the *New Orleans Times-Picayune* expressed fears that the $2 million allotted was insufficient for the construction of both auditorium and the larger parkway and plaza project. "The plan would be to proceed with the construction of the auditorium and if possible work on the parkway and beautification program in the future as funds permit."[10] Such concerns foreshadowed not only the immediate future of the project but the financial issues that would continue to plague projects planned for the area.

More immediately, the new auditorium highlighted New Orleans's entrenched segregationist policies. Like New Orleans's white community, the black community needed a large, modern facility to host black conventions. In fact, as the New Orleans tourist industry developed in the 1920s, many members of the white community, including the Association of Commerce, supported the idea of hosting black organizations, which would bring in money that was just as good as money from white conventioneers.[11] However, other boosters frowned on the idea of accommodating blacks for fear of upsetting white visitors. Moreover, to have blacks and whites mingling in the streets and in public facilities threatened New Orleans's social order. The issue of hosting black tourists occasionally played out publicly. When the use of Municipal Auditorium entered the equation, the Association of Commerce sided with the city's conservative elite. In fact, in the 1930s, the association regularly argued against hosting black conventions, contending that no facilities were available.[12] In the late 1930s, the National Association for the Advancement of Colored People unsuccessfully sued to desegregate the auditorium, and for decades, the subject of the auditorium remained intertwined with issues of race. In 1953, the auditorium became one of New Orleans's first integrated facilities when it hosted a United Negro College Fund Mardi Gras ball, but New Orleans mayors DeLesseps "Chep" Morrison Sr. and Victor Schiro subsequently denied civil rights groups access to the auditorium.[13]

Although the rest of the civic center and parkway project were never constructed, the idea of grouping public buildings remained a dominant development theme in Tremé for the next sixty years. The same Harland Bartholomew report that promoted the civic center also offered suggestions for maintaining the historic character of the Vieux Carré, among them an ordinance proposing French Quarter protections and supporting recommendations from the Vieux Carré Commission and American Institute of Architects.[14] The clearance of part of the French Quarter for the civic center apparently was not incompatible with the French Quarter's preservation.

POST–WORLD WAR II

During World War II, U.S. cities continued to decay. Prior to the war, localities had made considerable progress improving drainage and sanitation systems, but the condition and availability of housing waned until some New Deal legislation sought to address the country's public housing deficiencies.[15] After the war, middle-class families and their tax dollars moved to the suburbs, leaving urban poor residents with substandard housing, crumbling infrastructure, and even fewer resources. Through programs mandated by the U.S. Housing Acts of 1949 and 1954, the federal government began to clear slums to create new housing, parks, green spaces, and other public facilities.

Although these programs originally sought to revive American cities by improving the living conditions of the poor, creating a climate suitable for investment was the more important outcome of state-funded urban renewal programs. The federal government's financial commitment to the health of urban areas encouraged state legislators and local politicians to secure their fair share of development money by creating projects where federal money could be applied. Those projects displaced thousands of urban residents and destroyed countless historic structures and businesses.[16] In large cities, displaced residents found themselves relocated into public housing projects.

Chep Morrison, New Orleans's first reform mayor, oversaw many of the city's greatest changes. A World War II veteran, Morrison gained national media attention by aggressively and effectively implementing the development ideas of others, specifically the previous administration's ideas for a union passenger terminal, Robert Moses's highway projects, and the concepts of former city planner Brooke Duncan.[17] In the process, Morrison's initiatives displaced thousands of the city's black residents and failed to relocate them.[18]

Postwar New Orleans clearly needed some type of housing program. According to a 1952 housing report prepared for the Planning and Zoning Commission, "The preliminary releases of the 1950 housing census revealed that there were then some 65,676 occupied substandard dwelling units within the city—an increase of 24,950 units (58%) during the past ten years. Of particular importance however is the fact that the 1950 census revealed that approximately 63% of these substandard living units were occupied by nonwhite families. Clearly, there is an immediate local need for extensive slum clearance and urban redevelopment."[19] But from the first redevelopment initiatives of 1949 to the early 1960s, New Orleanians blocked the implementation of urban renewal programs that proposed creating private market housing.

Shortly after the report's release, however, the state of Louisiana passed legislation, introduced by representatives of New Orleans, denying any city the right to decide whether to implement an urban renewal program.[20] In addition, in 1954 the Louisiana legislature passed a law preventing New Orleans from using federal funds to clear or replace slums with private market housing. Many people, particularly members of the business community, believed that urban renewal was un-American, unpatriotic, and communist.

After unsuccessful attempts to amend the law in 1955 and 1956, the city finally implemented an urban renewal program in the early 1960s, using a loophole in the 1954 law. The loophole also cleared the way for the civic center project planned for the Tremé neighborhood, albeit under a different name.

When Morrison revived the civic center project, he relocated it several blocks away, in the Uptown back o' town area. The civic center's relocation was in name only; the city still desired a public buildings complex in the vicinity of Municipal Auditorium. The complex would now be focused on serving the city's cultural arts and entertainment needs. The city's postwar master plan, also written by Harland Bartholomew, supported the need for cultural facilities. The plan's "Preliminary Report, Public Buildings" found New Orleans's existing cultural and assembly buildings to be widely scattered and suggested grouping the buildings by function in four locations. For the assembly group, the report recommended a sports exposition building to supplement the Municipal Auditorium. Moreover,

> the problems involved in the planning and construction of major streets, parking, and public building in the vicinity of Beauregard Square are so closely interrelated that detailed planning of all these facilities must be carefully coordinated. Piecemeal design of the component improvements could easily destroy the workability of the overall plan or make its execution so expensive as to be wholly impracticable. The entire area should be developed as a single unit. Since a large amount of clearance is involved it might be logical to include the proposed improvements in a large-scale urban redevelopment project which would also embrace an additional area of deterioration north and west of the proposed assembly center.[21]

The report thus alluded to the financial issues that had plagued the original civic center and foreshadowed the problems that the assembly center/cultural center would experience.

The city made no real progress toward the construction of an assembly center until it initiated the capital budget program in 1955. By 1960, the city had spent $1.5 million to acquire land for the assembly center. Although funds were consistently appropriated for the assembly center, not all parties inside or outside the government were pleased with the project's progress. New Orleans's governmental watchdog, the Bureau of Governmental Research (BGR), noted the project's lack of direction, recommending in both 1958 and 1959 that the proposed bond election for the assembly center be turned down because of the lack of planning in spite of the proposal's good points, which included rising land costs, the need for parking, and the potential benefit and stimulus for the tourist and convention trade.[22] The BGR ultimately blasted the city because the sketchy project had not been subject to a public hearing and was not part of the master plan for the city's physical development.[23] Similarly, between 1958 and 1961, the City Planning Commission refused to include the assembly center in its capital program, pointing out the lack of planning as well as the need to secure federal funding.[24]

To satisfy calls for a development plan, the City Planning Commission presented the *Public Buildings Report II*, which dealt primarily with the cultural and international centers. The report's authors focused specifically on stimulating tourism and improving entertainment opportunities with new development and public assembly facilities and believed that the cultural center could "promote a nucleus for recreation, entertainment and culture in New Orleans and ultimately a high density dwelling area in the core of the city." The document recommended that the cultural center include, among other facilities, the existing Municipal Auditorium; an opera house seating four thousand; a concert hall seating twenty-five hundred; a legitimate theater seating between five and six hundred; a museum; a community facilities building; parking for two thousand cars; outdoor areas for exhibits, musical presentations, and carnival ceremonies; apartments; and restaurants, lounges, shops, schools, and churches.[25]

After the release of the public building report, the civic center/assembly center was no longer seen as the targeted site for conventions. That purpose was to be reassigned to or shared by the International Trade Mart, which the city had constructed, along with the International House, during the 1940s and which included exhibit space and conference rooms.

To accompany the newly developed plans, the city sought to fund the center with urban renewal funds, to which it had recently gained access. In 1964, the city committed $1.7 million to acquire the land bounded by North Villere, Dumaine, North Liberty, St. Ann, Marais, Orleans, and Basin Streets for the cultural center, assuming that the federal government would refund the money. The city then began the process of relocation and slum clearance.

Officially, 122 families (121 of them nonwhite) lived in the project area and needed to be relocated. Ninety of those families qualified for relocation into public housing based on income and family size. In addition, the area had 7 nonwhite property owners, all of whom desired to purchase new homes even though 5 were eligible for public housing. Those 90 families likely were placed in the Fischer Homes development, completed in 1965, on the West Bank of Orleans Parish community of Algiers.

Urban scholars writing about New Orleans have downplayed the significance of slum clearance in the city's modern development history. Michael P. Smith and Marlene Keller, for example, have suggested that the demolition of a "gray area" for a civic center was an acceptable and desirable act, citing a statement by James Jones, who financed the construction of the Superdome, that Mayor Morrison, a "visionary," had "successfully exorcized a wretched slum and replaced it [with] a civic center complex, thereby raising the value and attractiveness of adjacent land. The subsequent addition of office buildings, apartments, and hotel structures confirmed the wisdom of municipal regeneration."[26] Similarly, Richard Moe and Carter Wilkie claim that in Tremé, the "bad planning decisions that erased historic streets and ruined neighborhoods for elevated expressways still catalyze the preservation movement here. Claiborne Avenue, for instance, the traditional path of black Mardi Gras parades, was all but wiped out by an overhead expressway. Still, New Orleans has escaped much of the physical damage seen in other cities. Though some areas were cleared for new public housing developments during the depression, New Orleans shows few scars from postwar urban development."[27] In general, observers have contended that New Orleans's low-income, predominantly black communities suffered less from twentieth-century urban renewal than did comparable populations in other cities. Nevertheless, regardless of how many New Orleanians were actually displaced, the process was a significantly disruptive force. Moreover, the policy was implemented without adequate input from or consideration for the community residents.

On 22 July 1965, the city held a public hearing on the relocation process. Forty people attended, including city employees, administrators, and Christopher J. Bellone, the relocation officer. Bellone announced the existence of a full-time relocation office at 1202 St. Ann Street, staffed with a caseworker and housing inspector. According to Bellone, "Families and individuals will become eligible for relocation benefits if they live within the cultural center site when the city government and federal government enter into and sign a Loan and Grant Contract." Bellone emphasized that residents need not move immediately. At the meeting's conclusion, interested parties were permitted to comment on the project. Only six people spoke, and none expressed opposition to the plan. Most of the comments addressed appraisal values, leasing concerns, and property repairs. However, two persons offered illuminating comments concerning relocation issues:

> Mrs. M. Fernandez — Mrs. Fernandez, a tenant at 1410 Dumaine Street wanted to know if she would have enough time to find a decent place to move. Mr. Bellone told her the city would notify her when the property had been purchased and the relocation staff would offer every assistance in finding new quarters for her. She then wanted to know if she could start looking at the present time. Mr. Bellone told Mrs. Fernandez that she would not be eligible for any relocation payments if she were to move now. He advised her that if she wanted to take advantage of the grants she would have to stay on the premises until the loan and grant contract was signed.

Mike Cusimano — Mr. Cusimano voiced a complaint as to instructions to tenants in the area, citing his own rental property as an example. He said many of his
tenants did not comprehend what was told them and consequently they moved
and he has had difficulty renting his units. [Bellone] cited letters sent to area occupants and personal contacts made in the area.[28]

These comments suggest that many Tremé residents left the area before the
contract was signed and thus received no relocation assistance from the city.
The federal and local governments apparently met their legal obligation to no-
tify and relocate residents, but such efforts may not have been sufficient. The
area's poor black residents may not have been aware of the hearing, which was
advertised in the *New Orleans States-Item*, and may not have trusted the government's promises that relocation assistance would be provided if residents
waited to leave.

Following the clearance, the cultural center land sat vacant for several years
because the city lacked funds to construct the complex's buildings. During that
time, the plan was again tweaked in response to the suggestion that the cultural
center be modeled after New York City's Lincoln Center, the epitome of the
era's movement to construct cultural centers to showcase the performing arts,
a common feature of urban renewal programs. Lincoln Center, its performance
halls, and nearly five thousand apartments were constructed on fourteen acres
of Manhattan slum property. The fifty-three-acre slum project, which eventually cost $161 million, displaced seven thousand families and eight hundred
businesses.[29]

New Orleans's cultural center received an $8 million boost in 1968, with $4.5
million of that money earmarked for the construction of the complex's first
cultural building. In 1969, however, plans to construct the cultural center encountered another obstacle when the city was forced to reject all construction
bids because they came in over the amount allocated for construction.[30] The
building's construction finally began in 1971. Two years later, the civic center/
assembly center/cultural center project came to a close with the completion of
the Theater for the Performing Arts.

NEGROES IN THE DARK

In many ways, New Orleans's urban renewal experience mimicked the experiences of other large cities, with the displaced being predominantly African
American and the landlords mostly white and absentee. Within a local context, however, events such as urban renewal can provide insight into a city's

ideas about economic development, tourism, and race relations. The discussions surrounding the cultural center project, like the conversations regarding the Municipal Auditorium decades earlier, considered the potential for racial mixing along with other factors. The citizen who figured most prominently in discussions about how the cultural center would progress was a wealthy white businessman, Edward B. Benjamin; he and his wife, Blanche, held prominent positions within the city's arts organizations. Edward Benjamin served as an officer in New Orleans's Opera House Association and headed a community concert association, while Blanche Benjamin was the symphony's vice president. On 18 December 1962, Edward Benjamin expressed concern for the development of segregated arts facilities based on a belief that in the future, the city's "negro" element "will use the different auditorium facilities for all-negro events." Benjamin feared "that if there are white audiences in the other auditorium facility or facilities, and parking is not separate, then whites will be reluctant to co-mingle with thousands of negroes in the dark."[31]

Benjamin's comments echoed those of the commerce association in the 1930s. By the 1960s, however, political changes made the potential for racial mixing more pressing and whites increasingly vocal. Beginning in the 1950s, blacks in New Orleans had challenged and defeated discriminatory ordinances, and by 1962, it was clear that the segregation of public facilities would be hard to maintain. The passage of the 1964 Civil Rights Act brought an end to legal segregation in the South. While whites increasingly made their homes in the suburbs, a fight ensued over the use of public spaces. With newfound access and influence to the political process, inner-city blacks organized to repair their communities after decades of neglect.

By the early 1970s, after suffering great losses from the cultural center project, the black residents of Tremé began to make demands of the city. In the fall of 1971, City Planning Commission members came to accept the idea that a playground should be added to unused cultural center land. At a spring 1972 meeting between local and state officials and Tremé residents, residents learned that funds were available for community development. Harold Katner, director of the City Planning Commission, told attendees, "We feel we can get some money from the cultural center and the department of the interior for improvements in the area." State senator Adrian Duplantier offered his support, saying, "I am gratified to see a neighborhood fighting to preserve itself."[32]

Duplantier was alluding to efforts by the Tremé Community Improvement Association (TCIA), the first and arguably most important of the many Tremé community groups that have formed to fight against perceived neighborhood injustices. The TCIA was cofounded by James Hayes and Ron Chisom in 1969 and evolved to address unemployment and blight. In 1972, the TCIA boldly demanded 50 percent of the new jobs generated by the cultural center as a sort of reparation for the displaced residents. Central to the TCIA's request was a claim that New Orleans's relocation agency had been negligent in its executing federally funded effort to relocate and compensate the families displaced by the project. The city defended itself with the assertion that Tremé residents had "jumped the gun" in moving and that bureaucratic red tape had slowed the city's relocation efforts. The TCIA was also troubled by the loss of historic landmarks, voting strength, and the possibility of further displacement of the area's tenant-based population as a consequence of increasing rent and changing land uses. Local and state officials pledged to tap available development funds for physical improvements for the area and to assist residents in their fight against zoning changes.[33]

While members of the community may have wanted jobs, the most controversial outcome of their involvement was the intensely debated recreational facility. The origins of the facility are not clear, but money appropriated by bond issue for a recreational center in the general area of Tremé, North Claiborne, and St. Bernard was available to the New Orleans Recreation Department. During the spring of 1972, the city's planning and recreation departments negotiated regarding possible locations for the facility.[34] On 14 March, Katner explained the planning commission's outlook on the cultural center to his assistant, William Rapp: "We are both aware that we can anticipate no major construction program in the Cultural Center area within the foreseeable future because of the limited fiscal picture of the city of New Orleans. Conversely it does not appear appropriate to leave the magnitude of property involved available and underused until financial resources of the city have improved. I therefore request that we give serious consideration to this proposal which has emanated from the neighborhood."[35]

CONCLUSION

The city's construction of Municipal Auditorium in 1929 and the Theater for the Performing Arts in 1972–73 bookend the era when public spaces were created for New Orleans's mostly white, middle-class, concertgoing crowd. Several development plans from that era would have created large public building complexes in Tremé, but only those two monumental structures were erected. Attributing the city's failure to construct the complexes as envisioned to a lack of money is overstating and oversimplifying an obvious fact. At the root of the failed plans lay New Orleans's eagerness to compete with other cities. Lost in the process were issues of fairness for neighborhood residents and respect for the area's cultural traditions and landscape. As architectural writer Monroe Labouisse observed in the early 1970s, "The main point to remember here is that the Cultural Center began as a planning concept and remained no further thought out for many years. Yet demolition of Tremé was ordered on this pretext."[36] The misfortunes of the Tremé community are only highlighted by the intensity and passion preservationists brought to the fight against development projects in other parts of the city.

CHAPTER FOUR

Killing Claiborne's Avenue

We will sell to you: we want your money. But we will not employ you
to sell to others; we will not even employ you to sell to your own kind.
More than that, you and your kind, when you come to buy from the
hands of others, may, at any time, expect discourtesies and insults.
Moreover, we will send agents of other races into your homes seeking
business and there, across your threshold, around your fireside, in the
presence of loved ones, you may expect the same kind of humiliation.
—*Merah Stuart*

During the 1960s, construction of the interstate highway system resulted in
roadways that spanned the American landscape and cut through major cities.
In many of these cities, planners took advantage of African Americans' marginal status to run highways through their neighborhoods, wiping out residential areas as well as business districts.[1] Among the casualties was New Orleans's
North Claiborne Avenue, at one time the retail spine of Faubourg Tremé and
the Seventh Ward. In addition to serving the commercial needs of the local
community, Claiborne Avenue also served as a recreation and gathering space.
This consideration of Claiborne Avenue is not focused solely on the role of
Interstate 10 in the destruction of retail and cultural aspects of the area but also
discusses the creation of Claiborne Avenue in terms of New Orleans's larger
economic and geographic transitions, particularly the city's involvement in the
intensification of Jim Crow segregation and later the civil rights movement.
In addition to detailing the policy aspects of Interstate 10's construction, this
chapter demonstrates that the lack of protest against interstate construction
by the Tremé and Downtown communities likely resulted from the highway's
relatively early planning and the local community leaders' involvement in other
civil rights concerns.

The decline of New Orleans's French Quarter and subsequent efforts to
save it have been linked to the destruction of large sections of neighboring

Faubourg Tremé.[2] One aspect of that decline, however, contributed positively to the cultural landscape of other parts of Tremé — specifically, the development of Claiborne Avenue as a business district, social space, and public sphere for New Orleans's Downtown African American and colored Creole communities. This development involved the shift of the French Quarter's business district to Canal Street. On the eve of the Civil War and for several years thereafter, New Orleans's business district was concentrated on Royal and Chartres Streets in the French Quarter. The area was also home to several of New Orleans's most important banks and hotels. As the nineteenth century came to a close, however, more and more of Royal and Chartres's important social and economic functions moved to Canal Street.

Canal Street is now one of New Orleans's grandest thoroughfares. At more than 170 feet wide, it provides both tourists and locals with access to the riverfront, the French Quarter, and the central business district while also serving as the site of New Orleans's largest hotels and a host of restaurants and businesses. Contrary to popular belief, Canal Street was never the site of a canal. The street was planned to accommodate an extension of the Carondelet Canal toward the river, which explains its width.[3] Canal Street is also noted for its historic role in separating the culturally and historically French Downtown sections of New Orleans from the Uptown American section. The street's function as a boundary is evident in the changes that street names undergo as they cross Canal. From Downtown to Uptown, Chartres becomes Camp, Royal becomes St. Charles, Bourbon becomes Carondelet, and so on. While the wide thoroughfare served as the boundary between the first and second municipalities in the first half of the nineteenth century, subsequent research has shown that Canal was not a strict dividing line between the French and American sections.[4]

The business district's move to Canal Street was foreshadowed by the relocation of D. H. Holmes's department store from Chartres Street to Canal Street during the 1840s. Research by Anne Mosher, Barry Kiem, and Susan Franques shows that by 1885, the Chartres/Royal Street business district had grown out to Canal Street as far back o' town as Tremé and Liberty Streets.[5] The area from Chartres to the foot of Canal Street was dedicated to wholesale and industrial uses associated with riverfront rail and shipping. The movement of French Quarter businesses to Canal Street should come as no surprise, given the growth of the upriver American sector and the city's creeping growth lakeward. Canal Street's most important changes occurred between 1880 and 1940, as the retail section consolidated with the aid of the automobile and mass transit.

By the close of this period, eight more department stores joined D. H.

Holmes on Canal Street. As in other cities, New Orleans's retail core also served other functions, supporting entertainment and service industries. In the vicinity of Rampart Street, for example, stood the Joy, the Saenger, and the Lowes/State Palace theaters. Three drugstores operated on the corner of Dauphine and Canal, no doubt associated with "the inordinate number of doctors and dentists found in the upper-story offices of the new Maison-Blanche [department store] and Audubon buildings."[6] These functions and the wide array of specialty shops scattered throughout the Canal Street retail area made the street "the social and cultural core for the entire city."[7]

Jim Crow's exclusion of African Americans from the developing Canal Street district bore directly on the development of Claiborne Avenue. In the years after *Plessy v. Ferguson*, legal segregation spread from railcars to other southern public accommodations and schools.[8] In New Orleans, whites restricted black patronage of Canal Street. For example, in 1897, the white community attempted to isolate prostitution in the area that would become the infamous Storyville. According to Alecia Long, "In creating Storyville, the city sought to separate respectable New Orleanians from prostitutes. In the process, city leaders implied a rough equality between its population of 'lewd and abandoned women,' both white and black, and the African Americans who lived, went to school, and worshiped in the neighborhood. The Story Ordinances placed people of color on a plane with prostitutes and other sexual sinners, both conceptually and in terms of physical proximity."[9] On Canal Street around the same time, "you rarely [saw] a black person in the main Canal Stores, and if you did, you also saw white shoppers making a wide path for her, their eyes following her like daggers."[10] A 1913 advertisement for the Success Restaurant and Confections, located at 1428 Canal, boasted that the establishment was "The Only Restaurant on Canal Street for the Accommodation of Colored People." African Americans were also prohibited from working in visible positions and alongside whites.[11]

Barring African Americans from conducting business and working in increasingly white areas spurred the creation of business districts catering to African Americans. In many cases, however, African Americans were not involved as business owners. Writing in 1940, Merah Stuart observed, "In most of the cities of large Negro populations there are so-called 'negro districts.' . . . On all these streets there are numbers of mercantile establishments owned and operated chiefly by people of Hebrew or foreign extraction catering largely to Negro trade. The number and volume of patronage and the capitalization of business establishments of this type exceed by far Negro business units in the same cities. Negro merchants engaged in the same lines of trade can offer only feeble competition to them."[12]

In New Orleans, South Rampart Street, on the Uptown side of Canal Street, developed as the retail district that served African Americans. During its heyday, South Rampart provided nearly all of the goods and services required by African Americans living in the area variously known as the Battlefield, the Third Ward, or Uptown Back o' Town. Contrary to Stuart's contention, however, African American–owned businesses existed in significant numbers on Rampart alongside establishments owned by those of "foreign extraction," including Karnofsky's music store, owned by a Russian Jewish family that mentored the young Louis Armstrong.[13]

Stuart was no doubt aware of the Claiborne Avenue business district as well. At the time, the street was home to several insurance offices. The 1922–23 business directory published by the Colored Civic League of New Orleans identified Claiborne as a "negro business section . . . below Basin" Street and listed Claiborne as a "negro place of interest."[14] The Claiborne Avenue district, located Downtown between St. Bernard and Orleans Avenues, mirrored the retail and entertainment functions of Canal Street and, with its double rows of mature oak trees, provided a parklike setting in which children and families could play and a shady spot in which people could wait for friends, rides, or streetcars. In time, North Claiborne Avenue became the heart of Faubourg Tremé.

The fact that a business district formed on Claiborne Avenue should come as no surprise. Claiborne mirrors Canal in two ways. First, both streets are uncharacteristically wide, even by New Orleans standards. At 191 feet across, Claiborne provided an efficient corridor for travel from the Downtown wards to Canal Street. Furthermore, Claiborne's wide neutral ground proved a convenient location for public transportation. The origins of Claiborne Avenue as a business district, however, are somewhat ambiguous. Daniel Robert Samuels's research on the effects of Interstate 10's construction on the Tremé community and business district provides an idea of the services found on Claiborne and the role the street played in African American civil society in Downtown New Orleans. Samuels's interviews illuminate the institutions present on Claiborne Avenue and the role these institutions — most notably, insurance companies, funeral homes, and pharmacies, long considered the pillars not only of African American business districts but also of African American civil society — played in serving the Downtown neighborhoods.[15]

Evidence suggests that significant business activity existed on Claiborne Avenue before it developed into a full-fledged business district. One of the first prominent early businesses on North Claiborne was the People's Benevolent (later Industrial) Life Insurance.[16] The precursors to African American insurance companies were church relief societies, fraternal benefit societies, and mutual aid and benevolent societies. These organizations were important nodes in the larger cultural landscape and contributed to the development of neighborhood identity, specifically through the performance of daily activities and rituals such as parading. The decline of benevolent and burial societies and the rise of insurance companies involves the growing sophistication of African American consumers and business owners and the effects of limited opportunities for African Americans in the white world. The fundamental flaw plaguing the operation of fraternal, church, and mutual aid societies was that they collected the same amount of money from each member to pay illness and death benefits for other members. Money was doled out to members in need regardless of how much they had contributed. While this method of compensation was better than having no protection at all, it was not necessarily fair. When young, healthy members realized that they paid disproportionately more than did older members, younger people left or stopped joining, causing these societies to collapse. Insurance companies stepped into the resulting void.[17]

The transition to and development of insurance companies was often slow. Some societies became chartered and/or incorporated as mutual or joint stock companies, and early successes were copied by other industries, including mortuary businesses. Rhodes Enterprises, which presently performs funeral services and provides insurance, was started in 1884, when Duplain Rhodes Sr. migrated from Thibodaux to New Orleans. Rhodes, who supported his family by hiring out a cart for miscellaneous hauling, began performing burial services for African Americans. In 1928, Rhodes allied his company with a burial association to assist customers in paying for funeral expenses. In the early 1940s, Rhodes began acquiring the African American business of several white insurance companies. In the 1950s, Rhodes, at that time an Uptown operation, opened a funeral home on North Claiborne.[18] Similarly, another prominent New Orleans provider of funeral services, Gertrude Geddes Willis, originated in 1873 when Clem Geddes, a Creole from rural Louisiana, established a mortuary business; his son, Clem J. Geddes, started a burial association in 1909.[19]

Samuels attributes the origin of African American insurance businesses to white insurance companies' refusal to write policies for African Americans.[20] In New Orleans and many other places, however, few, if any, colored undertaking businesses existed before 1895, when whites served both communities. According to Rhodes, burial preparations for African Americans often occurred in horse stables. Maintaining separate accommodations evidently became an expensive proposition for whites, and African Americans began to enter the field, often with little objection from whites. By the first quarter of the twentieth century, however, African American funeral businesses came under attack from other African Americans for their visible displays of wealth.[21]

If whites were happy to share the burial business with African Americans, the same cannot be said for the insurance business. During the late nineteenth century, white-owned insurance companies provided coverage to African Americans, but when African American firms began to enter the field, competition resulted. According to Stuart, rude and inappropriate behavior by white agents aided the development of the African American insurance industry:

> Their haughtiness, discourtesies, and not infrequent abuses of the privacy of the home were resented but to great extent tolerated until the organization of negro companies into this field. Nothing has more greatly aided negro agents in meeting the competition of their more experienced competitors than the abundance of examples of insults and abuses of negro policy holders at the hands of white agents. . . . Other instances of the deliberate violation of the privacies of boudoirs and bathrooms over the protests and to the embarrassment of the female inmates have been bitterly and publicly resented by negro agents.[22]

In New Orleans, specific action by the white insurance industry played an important role in the creation of the city's first African American insurance companies. In 1906, larger white insurance firms began to suffer from competition at the hands of smaller providers operated by both African Americans and whites. New Orleans tradition dictated that doctors and medical societies offered insurance to patients and others on a small scale. White insurance companies successfully lobbied the Louisiana legislature to pass a law requiring a five-thousand-dollar cash deposit from all doctors, medical societies, and insurance companies operating in the state. The move, which proved devastating to African Americans, inspired Aristide Dejoie to bring together the existing Philadelphia, International, and George D. Geddes burial relief societies to form Unity Industrial Life Insurance.[23]

It is unclear whether People's Industrial Life Insurance or any of the other early Claiborne Avenue life insurance companies, including Standard Life Insurance, started as burial or burial relief organizations. What is certain is that the presence of insurance companies in African American business districts provided a catalyst for the development of ancillary services and businesses and for the employment of a newly created African American professional class. In addition to burial and funeral services, doctor's offices and pharmacies can be considered ancillary industries of insurance. Insurance companies often employed doctors, and a correlation exists between the locations of doctor's offices and those of drugstores and/or pharmacies. In 1915, Walter Cohen, founder of People's Life Insurance, opened People's drugstore at 624 South Rampart, a block from Unity Life Insurance in the Uptown African American business district. Cohen wrote to Booker T. Washington that the drugstore "is situated on a street where more colored population pass than any other in the city."[24] Unity's president, Paul Dejoie, son of Aristide and the first African American to pass Louisiana's medical boards, also opened drugstores. On North Claiborne, the Labranche pharmacy opened in the 1920s, and the Reed drugstore opened in the 1940s. These businesses provided African Americans with medical and health care services to which white businesses offered little access. Furthermore, these industries provided employment for a newly educated class of African Americans. This same group, as Adam Fairclough notes, formed the core of the New Orleans chapter of the National Association for the Advancement of Colored People (NAACP): "Growing out of neighborhood-based benevolent societies that furnished health care, sickness pensions, and funeral benefits, the insurance companies became the most important black-owned businesses in Louisiana. At a time when there were only 1,600 Negro-owned businesses in the entire state, when Louisiana had only two or three black lawyers, and when the census identified only 656 blacks in New Orleans as professionals or semiprofessionals, the significance of the insurance industry as a source for race leadership can scarcely be overstated."[25]

Despite the insurance industry's importance to the Downtown African American community, business and otherwise, it remained an elite enterprise. Even a common insurance agent was considerably better off than the laboring African Americans, Creole or not, who comprised the neighborhood. The stories of Tremé and Claiborne Avenue, however, are not elite. The neighborhoods straddling North Claiborne Avenue had always been home to members of the working class and for much of their history were quite mixed. These people shopped and played on Claiborne Avenue. Therefore, most of the business entities there catered to the community's specific needs for food, clothing, and entertainment. The combination of these activities, in addition to transportation functions, made African American districts in New Orleans and elsewhere hubs of activity.

North Claiborne was lively in the way that any business district is lively, with people hurrying about their business, shopping, and transitioning onto and off of public transportation. In a sense, these areas reflected the more flamboyant aesthetics of African American culture. The marginal status of African Americans seemed to amplify the "see and be seen" aspects that all downtowns foster. According to New Orleans jazz great Sidney Bechet, a Downtown Creole born in 1897, after starting in different parts of the city and stopping at different locations for drinks, bands participating in parades "would be moving to the meeting place. And the people they'd be up by Claiborne Avenue and St. Philip. They knew you'd be coming there. You *had* to pass some time. It was a parade and you'd be going to where the people were because naturally if you have a parade you were going out to be seen."[26] By the 1920s and 1930s, Dumaine Street had become part of the business hub. Jazz guitarist and historian Danny Barker recalled the corner of Dumaine and Claiborne as "one of the most famous corners in New Orleans. Dumaine and Claiborne, Dumaine and Robertson [one block south]: these were swinging corners."[27] Rock and Roll Hall of Fame drummer Earl Palmer, who grew up in Tremé, similarly remembered Claiborne and Dumaine as the site of the Chattard Brothers barbershop and Big Al Dennis's shoe shine stand, both of which served as local meeting places.[28]

Claiborne Avenue's neutral ground also provided African American children, who were excluded from most of the city's recreational spaces, with a place to play. According to a 1929 report on public recreation facilities, African Americans had access to only one playground, the Thomy Lafon Playground, located Uptown at Magnolia and Sixth. The report's authors argued that the absence of playgrounds forced African American children to "play in the streets, on the railroad tracks and on the levees. Adults seeking outdoor recreation are forced to go out of the city for their diversions, picnics and the like. The absence of opportunities for healthful outdoor play is one of the reasons for the large amount of delinquency found in the colored sections."[29] The Claiborne neutral ground, then, filled the park and playground needs of the Downtown neighborhoods.

The neutral ground also provided space for the practice and performance of cultural traditions unique to New Orleans's African American community. On Mardi Gras, the Claiborne neutral ground hosted African American carnival celebrations. Families gathered under the oak canopy to picnic and witness traditions excluded from mainline Mardi Gras, including the Zulu Social Aid and Pleasure Club parade and other characters of black Mardi Gras, including Indians, skeletons, baby dolls, and gold diggers.

While Claiborne Avenue of the 1950s bustled with local business traffic, the street's larger purpose — funneling auto traffic in and out of the French Quarter and the central business district — was beginning to falter. The city's newly created suburbs began to generate more Downtown road traffic. In addition, before the creation of the suburban shopping center, Downtown shopping was at its height, creating congested streets and threatening to choke off commerce. To remedy the traffic situation, the city began planning transportation changes that would forever alter Claiborne Avenue.

In a classic and relatively early attack on the interstate highway program, A. Q. Mowbray lists the criteria for routing decisions: "First choice is park lands and creek beds, since the land is cheap and flak comes from politically impotent bird watchers and petunia planters. Second choice is slum areas, which usually means Negro ghettos, since the land is relatively cheap, and the flak comes from politically weak black residents."[30] Most of the interstate highway literature states that planners and engineers were simply doing their job in routing roads through slums. Planners of the time are on record as saying that their training advised them to put roads through slums. Raymond Mohl, however, describes higher-level government officials who explicitly intended to use highway construction as a means of de facto slum clearance and urban development.[31]

Thomas MacDonald, head of the U.S. Bureau of Public Roads from 1919 to 1953, and Henry Wallace, U.S. secretary of agriculture from 1933 to 1940, were among the foremost proponents of this approach. Wallace told President Franklin D. Roosevelt that unsightly, unsanitary, and depreciating areas in inner cities could be cleared through the process of land acquisition for highway construction. For his part, MacDonald commented, "It is a happy circumstance that living conditions for the family can be re-established and permit the social as well as economic decay at the heart of the cities to be converted to a public asset."[32]

Not surprisingly, road building and construction interest groups also supported the use of roads to clear slums. These groups included state highway departments, the Urban Land Institute, the American Road Builders Association, and the automobile lobby. Race was often not mentioned explicitly, but because of African American migration to formerly white northern urban centers, "When highwaymen talked about clearing out central-city blight in the postwar era, everyone knew what they meant. The intent, the goal, was clear to most, even if it was rarely stated directly. Their intentions were clear from their statements, actions, and policies — and the visible consequences of the highways they built are the best evidence of their intended goals."[33]

Following the 1956 passage of the Interstate Highway Act, construction proceeded unfettered. Engineering logic, with the support of politicians who recognized the projects' economic benefits, guided the process. Many of the new roads carved through scenic countrysides and urban neighborhoods. Like most major cities, New Orleans was very concerned with traffic and the state of its roadways. The City Planning and Zoning Commission periodically released street reports detailing, among other things, current street conditions and proposed changes, including width, paved status, and presence of streetcar tracks. In 1946, the state of Louisiana released a proposal for New Orleans's streets developed by innovative New York urban planner Robert Moses. Moses's *Arterial Plan for New Orleans* suggested the construction of an elevated expressway along the Mississippi riverfront that would relieve surface congestion and facilitate dock functions.[34] The report was prepared with knowledge of New Orleans's preservation ethos, particularly as it concerned the French Quarter. Moses addressed those concerns by touting the need to integrate the Quarter with surrounding functions.[35] According to Richard Baumbach and William Borah, the Moses plan received little attention because of the city's preoccupation with consolidating its rail lines and constructing the Union Passenger Terminal under the guidance of Mayor DeLesseps "Chep" Morrison.[36]

In 1954, the city released another major street plan, this one featuring Claiborne Avenue as part of an interstate system that, where possible, made use of the city's public rights-of-way. According to Samuels, the Claiborne Avenue route presented two advantages: it was close to the central business district, and it could accommodate both an elevated expressway and the existing road.[37] The fate of Claiborne was seemingly sealed in 1956 when the city and state unveiled a detailed plan for road building prepared by the firm of Howard, Needles, Tammen, and Begendorf. The report, released within two months of the passage of the Interstate Highway Act, was completed as part of the process of securing federal highway funds.

In 1957, the new Central Area Committee produced a "Prospectus for Revitalizing the New Orleans Business District." The group sought to address the perceived decline of Downtown businesses and the related movement of businesses to the new suburbs. The report revised and elevated discussions about the problems of congestion, which, the group suggested, could be solved with interstate highways. The report advanced the increasingly common interstate design featuring inner and outer beltways, proposing the incorporation of Claiborne Avenue into this beltway system.[38] With engineering and planning officials and the business community throwing their weight behind transportation plans that included Claiborne Avenue as the site of an elevated interstate highway, the only way to stop the process was through the public meetings required as part of the Interstate Highway Act.

The first of two meetings was announced in the *New Orleans Times-Picayune* only hours before the gathering was to take place. That meeting was also scheduled for the morning, doubtless making it difficult for many area residents to attend. Much of the meeting was consumed with justifying the interstate's route, which basically followed the outline presented in the major street plan. The decision to route down Claiborne was discussed by W. T. Taylor, the state's assistant traffic and planning engineer, who noted that the plan satisfied several criteria—it was convenient for industry and undisruptive for residents. The meeting also included protests by the Gentilly and Lakeview residents who sought to cancel the Downtown bypass section of the interstate on the grounds that it would disrupt their neighborhoods. There is no record of anyone from Tremé or other Downtown areas arguing against the destruction of their neighborhoods.[39]

The first few years of the interstate construction process, which ultimately spanned from 1961 to 1969, were consumed by property acquisition. In July 1966, the Boh Brothers construction company received a contract worth nearly $7.4 million (about $10.14 million per mile) for the section of I-10 from St. Bernard Avenue to Orleans Avenue. Work began on 1 August, as the trees were removed from Claiborne Avenue's neutral ground. A 1961 *Times-Picayune* editorial had predicted, "It will take many years to heal the wound represented by the elimination of this grand-style reservation of open-park," though the article concluded that Claiborne's transformation for traffic purposes was "indispensable to general progress."[40] The section of Claiborne Avenue from Canal Street to Elysian Fields contained almost 500 oak trees. A Parks and Parkways Commission plan proposed relocating 51 of the 253 "inner" oaks at a cost of $125 per tree, while the 222 trees that lined the outer edges of the neutral ground were to be unaffected by the construction.[41] By the time the expressway was finished, however, few of the trees survived.

Construction of this section of the interstate lasted from October 1966 until April 1968. No buildings needed to be demolished for the roadway itself, since it ran over the Claiborne neutral ground, but three sets of ramps required the destruction of 125 structures that housed 170 residences and 50 businesses.[42]

More than thirty years later, area residents recalled that people had not fought the interstate because they received little or no notice of the project and because they perceived the change as inevitable. According to one man, Tex Stevens, "Now they had some blacks who said well, change got to come. [The interstate] had to go somewhere [and] decisions had already been made by the powers that be." Similarly, Theo Gosserand, who operated a printing company on Claiborne for four decades, commented, "You can't fight things like that. It was modernization that made this a ghetto, and nothing we could do would have made a bit of difference."[43] By the mid-1960s, however, coalitions of African Americans and whites delayed interstate construction in other parts of the country. In addition to directly petitioning lawmakers, these groups shaped "an intellectual and rhetorical climate that helped legitimate opposition to a program that was still generally popular."[44]

Even if interstates could not be diverted, locals could win housing concessions. Cities including Washington, D.C.; Baltimore; and Philadelphia fought construction of interstates through African American communities. But New Orleanians could muster little opposition for two reasons: the early timing of the Claiborne Avenue project, and the peculiarities of New Orleans civil rights politics. The construction of Interstate 40 through Nashville, Tennessee, offers insight into similar events in New Orleans.

Like New Orleans, Nashville's interstate experience began in 1956, at the dawn of the interstate highway program, when the engineering firm of Clark and Rapuano unveiled an interstate network design for the area. As part of that plan, Interstate 40 would enter the metropolitan area from the east, just as Interstate 65 did from the south, along rail tracks and yards, before connecting with the inner loop that surrounded the central business district. As proposed, I-40 would have crossed the path of only a few white-owned businesses, but opponents succeeded in substituting an alternate route through African American North Nashville that Mowbray described as "wip[ing] out Negro homes and churches, slic[ing] through a Negro college complex, and run[ning] along the main business street for 16 blocks, wiping out all the negro-owned businesses on one side of the street and isolating those on the other side from their customers. Some 650 homes, 27 apartment buildings, and several churches would be pounded into rubble. Isolation of the ghetto would be increased by the creation of fifty dead end streets."[45] The changes were made in May 1957 as part of a process that was unannounced to the public.

The alternate route received federal approval in 1958, but the project inexplicably remained dormant for nearly a decade. By the time the final route became public as part of the bidding process, the I-40 Steering Committee fought the destruction of North Nashville. The group's challenges eventually landed before the U.S. district court and the U.S. court of appeals; the courts agreed that the process was deficient and deleterious to the African American community but refused to halt or delay the project on the grounds that racial discrimination could not be proven. Despite the efforts of the NAACP Legal Defense and Education Fund, the U.S. Supreme Court refused to hear the case.[46]

Nashville's example demonstrates the ease with which African Americans could be excluded from the public decision-making process in the 1950s and 1960s. During the same years, behind-the-scenes planning for I-10 took place in New Orleans, and the same tactics that were used in Nashville were used in the Crescent City. But New Orleans's African Americans had success in resisting other unjust government policies and laws. In 1948, Creole lawyer A. P. Tureaud won a suit demanding that the New Orleans school board offer equal pay to African American teachers. Two years later, Tureaud introduced a school desegregation suit that reached the U.S. Supreme Court but was overtaken by the *Brown v. Board of Education* decision. In addition to their legal activism, New Orleanians took to the streets. In 1954, for example, residents boycotted an annual celebration that recognized the city's most noted education philanthropist, John McDonogh, but in so doing deprived more than thirty thousand schoolchildren of a day's education. Said organizer Revius Ortique, "The McDonogh Day incident was the first concerted challenge that color crossed all segments of the black community, and we spoke as one."[47]

One clear disadvantage for the African American community at the time of the public hearings was the absence of the NAACP. In 1956, the group's New Orleans chapter closed in response to the Louisiana legislature's decision to resurrect a 1924 law designed to stem the clandestine terrorist activities of the Ku Klux Klan by requiring the organization to reveal its membership lists. Instead of risking the safety of its members by revealing their names to white supremacist terrorists, the New Orleans NAACP ceased operations until the spring of 1961.[48]

By the late 1960s, when Nashville's African Americans and their allies were able to fight the interstate project, the process was too far along to be stopped. In New Orleans, however, no broad coalition protested I-10. Claiborne's business functions began to decline as soon as construction started because customers could no longer access those establishments. According to Roosevelt Steptoe and Clarence Thornton, "Minority businesses experience great hardships in relocating and often close when forced to move."[49] Local residents were clearly aware of the effects of long-term construction on the area. Commented Sybil Morial, widow of Mayor Dutch Morial, "When they were constructing it people were very upset because they didn't have access . . . , and those businesses were really dependent on walking and so forth; they were really suffering. I mean people stopped shopping there. They stopped coming, and I'm sure during the construction, that really killed it. I mean, you go six months without any customers because they can't get in, then your business is dead." More succinctly, in the words of Allison "Tootie" Montana, big chief of the Yellow Pocahontas Mardi Gras Indian tribe, "I-10 killed Claiborne St." Others believed that integration was the culprit: according to Langston Reed, son of the owner of Reed Pharmacy, "Integration, I think, was more of a catalyst to the change than the interstate. . . . I can remember going to my first white restaurant in

1965. . . . You were able to go into department stores and clothing stores and buy that which you were not privy to before . . . so now the black businesses had the white businesses to compete with."[50]

The simplest way to determine what actually killed Claiborne Avenue is to look at what happened to other African American business districts, including South Rampart, which was located less than a mile from Claiborne and which Walter Cohen identified as the busiest for African Americans.[51] They too suffered declines. Rudy Lombard, a civil rights movement veteran, insightfully noted, "Seems to me, the quintessential fact of it all was this high disregard and rude disrespect for the African American experience and the African American people . . . [b]y choosing a route that would take [the highway] straight down Claiborne Avenue. . . . [I]t was mean spirited in its conception to do it there . . . and it was only done there because these were essentially politically powerless people."[52] To paraphrase the law, African American people had no rights that white interstate planners had to respect.

Activists across the country eventually changed interstate construction policy. The passage of the Federal Highway Act in 1968 made residential displacement for the purpose of interstate construction illegal without the availability of decent replacement housing. In addition, displaced renters received additional money and time to find new homes. Compensation for business owners was also increased and extended. Almost ten years later, the Federal Highway administration announced its revised policy: "Locating highways where they will minimize disruption to residential neighborhoods emphasizes the stability of the neighborhood. Neighborhoods that may be particularly vulnerable to freeway disruption and therefore to be avoided are high-density, pedestrian-dependent neighborhoods with few autos available and strong racial or ethnic ties."[53] That description perfectly fit North Claiborne Avenue. But it was too late. As Mowbray commented, "To the uncounted hundreds of thousands thereby evicted the justice was like a reprieve for a man already hanged."[54]

The irony of the Claiborne Avenue story is inescapable and cruel. Homer Plessy was a product of Tremé, worshipping at St. Augustine and living for a time on Claiborne. He and other radical Creoles orchestrated the landmark case that bears his name and whose outcome codified segregation in the South, resulting in the creation of separate spaces for African Americans and whites and necessitating the development of places such as Claiborne Avenue and institutions such as African American insurance companies. But the legacy of Plessy and the radical Comité des Citoyens was reconstituted into a Creole-dominated NAACP, itself bolstered by professionals. Under the leadership of groups such as the NAACP and the Congress of Racial Equality, African Americans protested segregated Downtown businesses. Their victory led to the closing of business districts serving African American consumers and occupied, in many cases, by African American–owned businesses.

In addition, while neither whites nor African Americans took up the cause of Claiborne Avenue, the (white) preservation community began a heated and protracted conflict with the Central Area Committee, the planning commission, New Orleans mayor Victor Schiro, and the *Times-Picayune* to prevent the construction of an I-10 spur along the New Orleans riverfront. The conflict, known as the Second Battle of New Orleans, would be widely identified as the definitive battle between local communities and destructive federal projects. The controversy, which ended in a victory for the expressway opponents, occurred at the same time as the destruction of the Claiborne Avenue neutral ground and the subsequent construction of an elevated section of Interstate 10.

Preservationists won that battle by making a conscious effort to raise the controversy to the national level. One of the first and most productive moves came from a meeting between preservationists and Stewart Udall, secretary of the interior. Udall suggested that seeking National Historical Landmark designation for the Vieux Carré was the best way of proclaiming and protecting the area's integrity. Preservationists also took their cause directly to the national media, with letters and stories printed in the *Washington Post* and *Saturday Evening Post*.[55] The French Quarter eventually received the benefit of National Historic Landmark status, and the Second Battle of New Orleans ended on 1 July 1969, when the secretary of transportation canceled the project because of its predicted detrimental effect on the Vieux Carré.

The construction of the I-10 elevated expressway spurred action by the Tambourine and Fan Club, an African American cultural organization serving the Sixth and Seventh Wards. In 1970, the club began a dialogue with New Orleans officials, including representatives of the mayor's office and the Planning Commission, concerning revitalization and development for an area dubbed the Claiborne Corridor. The club sought to reinvigorate the area that had been adversely affected by the construction of I-10 only a few years earlier. The Louisiana Department of Highways made funds available for a feasibility study of "alternate plans for developing the public land underneath and adjacent to the I-10 corridor."[56] In 1973, the state authorized the Claiborne Avenue Design Team to begin the study. Three years later, the team, comprised principally of engineers and social scientists but also including activists, scholars, and other citizens, presented the *Claiborne Avenue I-10 Multi-Use Study*. The report included neighborhood histories and other points of historical interest for the area between Poydras, Peoples, Galvez, and Rampart/St. Claude, highlighting the damage to the area and justifying funding for improvements.

The study proposed an $80 million redevelopment project that included a realignment of Claiborne Avenue, changes to the existing ramps, and land acquisition as well as the creation of community facilities and beautification projects. The study also presented two less intensive alternatives, one for $72 million and another proposing mostly beautification and recreation for $10 million.[57]

By 1970, one of New Orleans's most important public spaces, at least for Downtown African Americans, had been destroyed. Perversely, the construction of an elevated rather than grade-level highway means that the physical space still exists. But most of the life and activity that once filled the area between the northbound and southbound lanes of Claiborne Avenue, now in the shadow of the highway, is gone. The "place" of Claiborne Avenue, at least as it had existed, has been lost forever.

CHAPTER FIVE

A Park for Louis

On 6 July 1971, renowned musician Louis Armstrong passed away in his modest Queens, New York, home, as a consequence of a massive heart attack suffered in his sleep. Born in New Orleans at the dawn of the twentieth century, Armstrong matured hand in hand with jazz music. When jazz migrated north from New Orleans, Armstrong followed, and he is arguably the most important figure not only in jazz but in all of American music. According to jazz and cultural critic Stanley Crouch, "The extent of [Armstrong's] influence across jazz, across American music and around the world has such continuing stature that he is one of the few who can easily be mentioned with Stravinsky, Picasso and Joyce. His life was the embodiment of one who moves from rags to riches, from anonymity to internationally imitated innovator. Louis Daniel Armstrong supplied revolutionary language that took on such pervasiveness that it became commonplace, like the light bulb, the airplane, the telephone."[1]

It is easy to understand, then, that Armstrong is the most important figure, living or dead, associated with New Orleans. In both song and print, Armstrong fondly recalled his youth in New Orleans, even though he grew up poor in a deeply racist and segregated society. Years later, however, perhaps after viewing the more tolerant world of the North and traveling internationally, Armstrong became disenchanted with the segregationist policies of the South, including New Orleans. In the later decades of his life, Armstrong refused to play in New Orleans because of its segregationist policies. As Dan Morgenstern has written, Armstrong had difficulty getting a "proper reception in [his] own home."[2] Since his relationship with his place of birth eventually seemed to heal, many people are surprised to learn that Armstrong is buried not in New Orleans but in Flushing Cemetery, near his home of nearly thirty years.

Unsuccessful in securing the return of Armstrong's body for interment in New Orleans, city leaders were nevertheless intent on memorializing their expatriate impresario. Shortly after Armstrong's death, New Orleans mayor Moon Landrieu assembled the Citizens Committee for a Memorial to Louis Armstrong. The group, comprised of planners, architects, jazz scholars and musicians, and community activists, was charged with conceiving a proper tribute to Armstrong's life. On 30 June 1972, the committee, cochaired by juvenile court judge and future mayor Ernest N. "Dutch" Morial and *New Orleans States-Item* assistant editor Charles Ferguson recommended that a park named in Armstrong's honor be constructed on the large swath of vacant land surrounding the Municipal Auditorium. Created with input from relevant parties, the new park would follow the mold of earlier New Orleans outdoor music venues and would be consistent with the surrounding area's musical heritage.[3]

The committee's considerations primarily involved Armstrong's impact on American music and the importance of appropriately honoring him and his accomplishments. Design suggestions included bandstands, schools of music, fountains, monuments, and the renaming of streets and buildings, "but again and again the suggestions pointed to the Cultural Center area, to Congo Square, to Cultural Building II, to Perseverance Hall, to Basin Street. It began to be obvious to each one of us that a park incorporating many of these suggestions was the only really appropriate memorial . . . and that the [unfinished cultural center] was the only really logical location."[4] Some of the suggestions were certainly legitimate, such as those that cited the area's association with jazz history as evidenced by the activities that took place at Economy Hall, the San Jacinto Club, and Hopes Hall, among others.[5]

The logic of siting the memorial at the cultural center is not that of memorials but of making sense of the debacle of the cultural center project. Points in favor of the park idea included the fact that "from the standpoint of financial feasibility, the area is already owned by the city. However, city officials tell us that because of the city's extremely limited capital funding picture, the large scale public buildings originally proposed for the area will not be built anytime in the foreseeable future. Turning the area into a park will put the land to public use as soon as possible." Moreover, "the area currently looks like a disaster area serving as a depressant to the Tremé community, [Vieux Carré] and [central business district], that the park would be a leisure destination for the same area and lastly that Bourbon Street, the city's only jazz mecca[,] was inappropriate as a family jazz attraction."[6]

At the time of the committee's decision, neither the cost of construction nor the source of funding for the park was known. Furthermore, there were no development plans. Mayor Landrieu saw the proposed park as complementing other development plans scheduled for Downtown, including the New Orleans Center shopping plaza and a Hyatt Regency Hotel across from the Superdome, the federal complex at Lafayette Square, the Pan-American Life Building, the Spanish Plaza, the development of Jackson Brewery, and the development of air rights over the riverfront.[7] These projects represented a shift in national economic development trends and local urban development priorities.

This chapter outlines the development of Armstrong Park from the early planning stages through the emergence of the issue of privatization in the 1990s, emphasizing the opposition raised by Tremé activists and members of New Orleans's African American community. The city's blacks were at odds with middle-class theatergoers and their vision of park development during the 1970s and with city leaders' and developers' vision during the following decade.

Armstrong's death, however, did not result in a clean separation of the cultural center project from the new plans. New Orleans's theatergoing crowd had recently tried and failed to ward off efforts by members of the Tremé community and the city to locate on the grounds of the cultural center a community center that would serve the surrounding neighborhood. Edward Benjamin's earlier concerns about segregated facilities undoubtedly reflected those of the larger cultural arts community. The demographic and electoral changes of late 1960s, however, recast the political landscape as one less responsive to New Orleans's white elite. The events surrounding the proposed changes in the cultural center plan mirror the city's general political transformations.

The Armstrong Park project gained support and momentum in April 1973. Early in the month, the Louis Armstrong Park Memorial Committee announced the selection of a heralded San Francisco urban design firm, Lawrence Halprin and Associates, as the park's planners. Under the contract, Halprin would receive fifty thousand dollars for developing a master plan for Armstrong Park.[8]

When Benjamin learned of this decision, he led the primarily white elite arts community in a heated protest against an Armstrong/jazz memorial. In June, Benjamin wrote that he found "preposterous" the idea of "designat[ing] the whole of Municipal Auditorium New Orleans theater area as Louis Armstrong Park." According to Benjamin, "Satchmo was only one of many great New Orleans Jazz musicians," and "his best riffs were jungle sound as compared with many magnificent hours of sight and sound over the two hundred year old history of music, opera, ballet, and theatre." Benjamin concluded that if the planning commission "persist[ed] in the proposed scheme you're going to make all of the administration look like panderers to the coloured vote and you will destroy your image with the public at large."[9] Benjamin thus ushered in a new round of complaints from theatergoers. Most of these complaints relegated jazz to a diminished status, somehow less than classical music and other cultural arts. Benjamin told Albert Saputo, chair of what Benjamin termed the Louis Armstrong Park Client Committee, that the call for a people's park was "crazy. It's like saying that Lincoln Center should be a 'people' park with a jazz orientation." Benjamin believed that "it's nonsense to equate the other performing arts with jazz or to slant the facilities of these performing arts to take jazz into account."[10]

Later in the summer, Benjamin argued that the "obsession" with honoring Armstrong could be sated by naming a jazz museum for Armstrong and locating it in the vicinity of the auditorium. Benjamin may have realized that characterizing jazz as inferior was turning out to be a losing strategy, but he nevertheless continued pleading his case to more like-minded audiences and asking those sympathetic to his view to join his chorus. In August, Benjamin wrote to Robert Manard, president of the New Orleans Area Chamber of Commerce, "I would like to see the Chamber of Commerce get into the act and oppose nonsensical diversion of the present cultural center and amusement park."[11]

Despite the detractors' concerns, the Halprin firm spent the summer of 1973 preparing a plan for the Armstrong memorial, a process that included conversations with community groups and businesspeople. By August, however, the Halprin proposal was generating negative sentiment, even though Mayor Landrieu had forbidden copies of the plan to be released for publication. Landrieu's attempts at secrecy suggest that individuals in the city administration were sympathetic to opposition groups' views. The Halprin plan's detractors basically contended that the firm's ideas would create a Disneyfied New Orleans, providing artificial entertainment for profit when the city had plenty of authentic attractions outside the park.[12]

The firm formally unveiled its design concept to the public on 12 September 1973. For the most part, the design corresponded with preliminary versions of the plan, except that the completed park plan included a Ferris wheel and an admission fee. Several groups immediately protested the deletion of previous components of the cultural center from the new plan and questioned which elements would and would not be inside the park fence.[13]

The dissenters actually came from two groups, theatergoers and those interested in the original plan's educational aspects. The theatergoers' concerns continued to focus on parking spaces and the naming of a place of "high culture" for an African American jazz musician. Complaints often employed culturally elitist and racist arguments. For example, concerned citizen Alfred Lozano wrote that Armstrong should be dropped from the cultural center's name. Instead, "all efforts to memorialize him should be directed to the establishment of an all-negro school offering a curriculum, to be determined by negroes only, that will, in their opinion, offer the most and best results for negroes. . . . [T]he culture relevant to the cultural center is none other than

HIGH culture of the High Civilized society of Whites who founded and built this city—the French, the Spaniards and the English. . . . The cultural heritage of New Orleans is HIGH and CIVILIZED, European and English. It is not Congolese. It is not Louis Armstrong." In another letter, real estate agent and appraiser Omer Kuebel argued that "Armstrong never did represent the Black Community of New Orleans, nor does his image offer any inspiration to those blacks who aspire to be educated, cultured and good citizens of this City. . . . He was never an ambassador for New Orleans—rather he typified a comic who struck it lucky, made a lot of money, lived in Chicago and New York and contributed nothing to the cultural uplifting of our Black citizens."[14]

More harsh criticism came from groups positioned to reap educational benefits from the cultural center—the Women's Auxiliary of the Chamber of Commerce and the Junior League. They took issue with the omission of the Museum of Science and Industry from the Armstrong Park plans and critiqued park planners' refusal to designate a school within the planned park boundaries to be converted for use as a school for the creative arts. These groups seemed unconcerned about the park as a tribute to Armstrong. Betty Wood, executive director of the New Orleans Sierra Club, opined, "A monument to Louis Armstrong in the form of a community park with facilities to educate and enrich the lives of the residents of the city would be of far more benefit than a commercial park established essentially for private gain." New Orleans arts patron Donald A. Meyer concluded, "The central focus of the entire area has now changed from a cultural and educational system to that of an amusement park, which appears to be operated by commercial interests who may have little if any connection with the educational community."[15]

The question of what belonged inside and outside of the park refers specifically to the locational fate of the Tremé community's recreation/community center facility. The Tremé community generally remained quiet during the Armstrong Park/cultural center debate. The Tambourine and Fan community group approved of the general idea of Louis Armstrong Park, while the Tremé Community Improvement Association (TCIA) approved of Halprin's original plan despite its provision for an admission fee. That some members of the Tremé community backed the plan suggests that after so much seemingly purposeless destruction, residents thought that the park had a future and might serve as a kind of cultural keystone. The community recreation center presented a different though related set of concerns. The Tremé community had originally conceived of the center as serving the recreation needs of local children. City and state officials supported the center's creation as a way to soften the impact of Interstate 10's construction. In addition, residents saw the recreation center as a good use of space that was no longer part of proposals for the cultural center. City official Harold Katner proposed funding the center with monies from the Department of the Interior and from the defunct cultural center project.[16] Much to Benjamin's chagrin, however, the center was added to plans conceived after the demise of the cultural center idea and was soon incorporated into the plan for Louis Armstrong Park. The recreation center became a political issue when several council members objected to Landrieu's attempt to move nearly $1 million from the capital budget to the center, which carried an original budget of $700,000. Several councilmen objected to the transfer of funds, but the measure nevertheless passed. As state representative Louis Charbonnet III put it, after all the displacement for the cultural center, "we have convinced the city administration to give us back some of that land."[17] Just as other interested parties had done, the Tremé community voiced its displeasure with certain aspects of the Halprin plan before its official release. Specifically, preliminary drawings placed the recreational center outside the park's iron gates, which community leaders perceived as an attempt to segregate them. Robin Riley, one of the park's architects, countered that locating the facility outside the fence would give the community unlimited access regardless of what was going on inside; moreover, the fence, he contended, was required for security purposes.[18]

Although the Tremé community remained displeased with details of the recreation center, it supported the official plan. The New Orleans Jazz Club, the New Orleans Jazz and Heritage Foundation, the Orleans Parish School Board, the Human Relations Committee, the Council of Arts for Children, the New Orleans Recreation Department, and the St. Mark's Community Center joined the Tremé community in support of the park plan. The issue became moot when the council decided to allocate funds for the center.[19]

A month after a controversial public meeting, the City Planning Commission approved the creation of Armstrong Park. To quiet opposition, the plan was scaled back, removing many of the amusement park components and adding parking spaces.[20] City council members, however, still offered considerable opposition to the "fake lakes" and several other minor issues.[21]

A major change in the park planning process happened in January 1974, when the city canceled Halprin's contract after the firm submitted final plans that were at odds with those approved by the council and planning commission. In addition, Halprin requested $140,000 for the work completed, when the agreement had been for $50,000. Instead of rebidding the project, the city decided to appoint Riley as the park's lead architect and designer. Riley, a member of the original Louis Armstrong Park Memorial Committee, had been designated the city's representative, working with Halprin. Riley's team subsequently developed a strategy for completing Armstrong Park in two phases, the first of which included "renovations to the jazz complex" and completion of the lagoon, Congo Square, the fence, parking, and general landscaping. The second phase would incorporate the private sector to make the park an attraction.

The last major hurdle to pleasing the Tremé community arose at the close of 1974. Facing another cost overrun, Landrieu sought five hundred thousand dollars in federal community development funds to complete the Tremé Community Center (previously known as the recreation center). Tremé residents cited distrust of Landrieu's administration as a reason to reject the idea, arguing that if the money were accepted, the community would lose control of the center to the New Orleans Recreation Department. After considerable debate, the community rejected the funds, concluding instead that the neighborhood's primary concern was to establish a homeownership program, particularly for black residents.[22]

The final obstacle to the completion of Armstrong Park's first phase was the parking issue, a major concern of theatergoers for a decade. The proposed plan for Armstrong Park called for an $8 million parking garage to be constructed near the completed park. A "coalition of patrons," led by Edward Benjamin and John Dodt, submitted a petition demanding that two thousand parking spaces be created on-site at the expense of at least some of the planned lagoons.[23] *New Orleans States-Item* columnist Jack Davis characterized the battle as "Armstrong Park vs. the Automobile." Foreshadowing future debates, Davis concluded, "The opposition has focused on the single notion that this valuable public space should be used to store the private automobiles of people who patronize the symphony, opera, and other cultural events. . . . It's distressing to see automobile storage treated as such an important question. If cities like New Orleans are to survive, it will be because we recognize the damage caused by the obsessive obeisance to the destructive needs of the private car."[24] Many saw the group's demands as racist, though Dodt objected, "How can people claim lagoons are black and parking is white?"[25] But fifteen years earlier, Benjamin had racialized the parking issue.

In defense of the argument for parking and against the lagoons, a coalition of arts organizations submitted petitions containing twenty-eight thousand signatures to the city council in an effort to have an election called on the matter, but the council nevertheless voted to allow development to proceed as planned. As a compromise, a certain number of parking spaces were to be maintained on-site until the construction of the off-site facility. The vote signaled the end of any substantive influence by the arts patrons on cultural center area planning and construction. When Armstrong Park opened four years later, the arts patrons' parking spaces were within the park boundaries.[26]

In the late 1970s, park construction pressed on, albeit at a slower-than-scheduled pace. The Louis Armstrong statue was completed in 1978 and was unveiled at Jackson Square. However, the statue was then warehoused until the park's opening in 1980. During this period, public debate about park planning discussions cooled, and discussions about the park again became the purview of city officials, who conducted their deliberations behind closed doors.

ARMSTRONG PARK — PHASE 2

The dedication ceremony for Armstrong Park took place on 15 April 1980, a fitting culmination of the highly anticipated and controversial eight-year, $10 million project. The mayor's executive assistant, Anthony Mumphrey, referred to the production as "the greatest free show on earth." The scheduled performers included international jazz stars Count Basie and his orchestra, Dave Brubeck, and Lionel Hampton. Local stars included Al Hirt, Dave Bartholomew, and Dejan's Olympia Brass Band. Also on hand were numerous gospel choirs, African dance troupes, jazz bands, Mardi Gras Indians, and second-line clubs as well as slide shows, films, and photographic exhibits.[27]

At the same time, however, the city was preparing for Phase II of Armstrong Park development, a process that did not involve the public. In the first months of 1978, the Special Task Force on Armstrong Park prepared a confidential report for mayor-elect Ernest Morial and the Office of Mayoral Transition. Morial, who had cochaired the original Armstrong Park committee, now had to deal with the entity that he had helped create.

The report provided a park history, an assessment of Armstrong Park's present condition, and recommendations for its future use. The report was predominantly negative and portrayed the park as deeply troubled as a consequence of its conceptual origins. The report attributed the park's problems to the lack of official oversight, the absence of a use plan, uncertainty concerning future management personnel, parking, funding, its relationship to other attractions, and its relationship with the Tremé Community Center. The report insisted that the park be an "attraction," but planners had few ideas for bona fide jazz-related features as well as few ways to fund such features without an admission fee. In fact, it was unclear how basic park upkeep would be funded. As the report suggested, "Absent a series of well coordinated attractions, this Park could rapidly decline into a trash-strewn dangerous site and hurt the Quarter and the Cultural Center (Theater for the Performing Arts)." The report thus suggested the creation of a "formal operating entity" with links to an existing operating budget. Also, an ongoing public relations/event planning component was deemed important to the park's long-term success. In addition, the report stressed the need for something to augment or complement the park's jazz motif, which the task force saw as an insufficient draw. The report's authors suggested an attraction based on black or Creole history, "highlight[ing] the common man's lifestyle — a type of 'red beans and rice' Gallier House." The key component of such an attraction would be artifacts excavated during construction of Phase I.[28]

The report also provides insight into the relationship between the Tremé neighborhood and the city via the Tremé Community Center. At the time of the report's release, the two-year-old center was already "a shambles."[29] The pool and the basketball court, among other facilities, were in serious disrepair, and staffing and upkeep issues plagued the center. The report blamed the situation on mismanagement by the New Orleans Recreation Department. Although the center was a wholly separate facility from the park, as community consensus had suggested, the task force saw the two as inexorably linked. Furthermore, the report encouraged the incorporation of the local black community into whatever permanent entity was created, because "with a black mayor in place, demands from the black community for an increased voice in park activities will be heard. [Blacks] should be incorporated into the policy body for the Park at the earliest possible date and the client committee expanded to permit this source of new ideas."[30] Indeed, members of the community had already begun to request control of parking contracts and would continue to make such requests based on the harm the community had suffered in previous decades.

In early April, just prior to the park's dedication, Mumphrey announced that the city had only enough money to provide cleanup and security for one year. The park's future management options and functions were assessed as part of a ninety-thousand-dollar study that would determine how best to make Armstrong Park financially profitable or at least self-sufficient.[31] In the fall of 1982, after receiving confirmation from the city attorney and the state attorney general that the leasing of publicly held land did not run counter to the law, the City of New Orleans formally opened the bidding process for Phase II development proposals.[32] During the remainder of the 1980s, the administrations of Mayors Morial and Sidney Barthelemy entertained several proposals to develop Phase II of Armstrong Park. Adversarial relationships between the occupants of the mayor's office and the city council, including long-standing personal animosities, at times complicated the process. Most significant, however, was the level of involvement by the leaders of the Tremé community and their success in influencing the process.

On 24 February 1983, after more than a year of reviewing Phase II development proposals, Morial selected the Armstrong Park Corporation, a local company, to develop and manage the park. The company's $96 million proposal included not only bars and restaurants but also hotels, which distinguished it from the other, much cheaper, bids submitted by professional attraction producer Tommy Walker Spectaculars and by Charbonnet. After an intense debate involving the Tremé community and the city council, the Armstrong Park Corporation's plan failed to win support, marking the end of the first round of Phase II development proposals.[33] Developers continued to submit plans for park development well into the next decade, however. In 1984, the city received two less intrusive, smaller-scale proposals. One, submitted by local lawyer David Fine and a group of investors, proposed focusing specifically on the promotion and preservation of jazz. Absent from the plan were the hotels, restaurants, and shops that had caused the Armstrong Park Corporation plan to be deemed too intensive. But both of the less-ambitious plans failed after the Morial administration refused its support.[34] The grand-scale plans returned in 1987 when another local developer proposed a $100 million entertainment center.[35] By that time, however, the city was looking toward another proposal to save Armstrong Park.

TIVOLI REVISITED

With Barthelemy's election as New Orleans's mayor in 1986, the complexion of the Phase II development process changed. As a city councilman, Barthelemy had been instrumental in defeating the Armstrong Park Corporation's proposal. In the spring of 1987, Barthelemy formed the Armstrong Park Committee, a group of government, business, and community leaders, to address the issue. In an effort to include the community in the planning process, activists Jim Hayes and Ronald Chisom were named as cochairs of the committee, which sought to develop a park that would attract people and create jobs without altering the community's character.[36] In addition to the fiscal problems and community concerns that dogged the park to that point, the park was also burdened by the aftermath of a tragic shooting. On 8 January 1987, an Ohio woman, Patricia Lobaugh, was shot to death in an attempted robbery as she snapped photographs in the park. The murder solidified the public's perception of Armstrong Park as a dangerous place.[37]

In October 1987, after a three-and-a-half-year hiatus from seriously entertaining Armstrong Park development plans, the city announced that it was courting the Tivoli Corporation, which oversaw Copenhagen's Tivoli Gardens, to complete the project. After initial discussions, the city sent a delegation, led by Barthelemy, to Denmark. The TCIA's Chisom also made the trip.[38]

Armstrong Tivoli Park, as it would be called, was designated "the city's top priority economic development project in the area of tourism" and would include a mix of amusements, attractions, concerts, restaurants, and gardens targeted at both tourists and locals. The master plan for the new park called for paid admissions as well as drastic changes to the park's physical design. Only Municipal Auditorium, the Theater for the Performing Arts, Congo Square, and the jazz complex would have remained the same. As a paid admission facility, the park would remain fenced. Free events could be held inside, however.[39]

The city presented the Tivoli project as an economically feasible endeavor, conservatively priced at $56 million. Notions that the park would provide "first class establishments" for jazz, increase international tourism, and change the city's adult-only reputation bolstered the economic justification. The park was also presented as a future employer of Tremé neighborhood residents in occupations ranging from construction workers to street musicians and vendors. Financing for the project was broken down into short-term, intermediate, and long-term segments. In the short term, funding was projected to come from a $20 million state commitment, with the remaining $36 million provided by the Section 108 loan guarantee program administered by the U.S. Department of Housing and Urban Development (HUD). Intermediate funding would come from the issuance of public stock. Finally, long-term funds for profitable businesses would come from the private sector.[40] Much like the Armstrong Park Corporation, the Tivoli plan failed in large part because of the Tremé community's opposition.

ARMSTRONG PARK — OPPOSITION

Tremé's rich history of community-based organizations and political activism was of little use in fighting the destructive urban development policies of the 1950s and 1960s. By the time preparations were being made to construct the elevated interstate over Claiborne Avenue and to construct the cultural center, the radical Creoles had long vacated Tremé and were residing in (or more accurately, identifying with) the Seventh Ward. At the time, politically active blacks were more concerned with securing their civil rights than with fighting to save a deteriorating neighborhood. As a result, Interstate 10 was constructed with little if any opposition.

The demographic and political changes of the late 1960s altered the nature of opposition launched by the Tremé community. Activists encouraged the government to fund programs and improvements to make the Claiborne Corridor a livable space. The damage had largely been done, and the community could suffer little else from the proposed improvements. With the Phase II development of Armstrong Park, however, insult could be added to the initial injury. The community's complaints about the proposed development fell into four basic areas: public access, minority businesses, management, and property values. Community members' most consistent concern throughout the process was the threat of exclusion from Armstrong Park based on a gate charge.[41]

Tremé activists used the park's grand-opening ceremony as a platform to utter their first public words of opposition to the completed park. Hayes told those assembled, "I think this park's beautiful, and I think most of you do, but I want you to remember that because of this park, a lot of black people suffered, and they're still suffering. . . . [S]omebody's going to pay for all this suffering."[42]

Park critics regularly issued similar remarks over the next decade. Four months after the dedication ceremony, with the Phase II development process under way, Hayes's comments became less caustic and more pragmatic: "If the Park is closed to the community, there could be some serious consequences. What happens if the kids have to pay twenty-five cents to get in? That's what we are worried about."[43] The threat became real after Morial approved the Armstrong Park Corporation's plan in the spring of 1983. Opposition came not only from members of the Tremé community but also from the city council, which had questions concerning the selection process. To address Tremé's concerns, the council created two subcommittees to study the proposals submitted by the Armstrong Park Corporation and others. One of the subcommittees was comprised of ten local residents and citizens; the second was a five-member group of city officials. The citizen panel rejected all three proposals, citing a lack of community representation in park management and dissatisfaction with the intensity of proposed development.[44] The committee based its decision on the belief that the proposed changes would destroy the park as it existed. The committee refused to approve any plan that would make the park a paid admission facility and that proposed changes outside of the cultural and architectural context of the neighborhood. In lieu of the proposed development, the citizens' subcommittee suggested that a nonprofit corporation govern Armstrong Park. But the city subcommittee, which submitted its report a month later, ignored the community's concerns and supported the Armstrong Park Corporation's bid. The recommendations of the city subcommittee were seen as a compromise between private development and community control. The committee suggested that negotiations between the Armstrong Park Corporation and the city be conducted by an advisory committee comprised of two council members, a Tremé resident, a representative from the mayor's office, and a member of the original Armstrong Park development committee. The report suggested a plan for Armstrong Park that reduced the intensity of development. Sixty percent of the park would be fenced, would require paid admission, and would contain restaurants, bars, performance areas, hotels, and other attractions. The remaining area would be less intensive and operate without an admission fee. A nonprofit corporation would advise the park in planning and management decisions.[45] The lone critic on the city committee was Councilman Sidney Barthelemy, who had publicly supported the citizens committee's findings. According to Barthelemy, "Tremé is somewhat of a low to middle income neighborhood and for people to have to pay $5, $6, $8 to get in—they would not participate at all."[46]

The full city council agreed with Barthelemy, voting in December to reject the Armstrong Park Corporation's proposal. Council members cited community concerns and the lack of control over the park after a long-term lease was signed. Barthelemy commented, "You don't create parks to make money. . . . [Y]ou create parks as a place for people to bring their families and have fun. We're losing sight of that concept with Armstrong Park."[47] The council's decision effectively ended the first round of Phase II development plans by preventing the mayor from entering into a leasing agreement with the Armstrong Park Corporation.[48] The courts brought some closure to the issue by ruling that the city council must be involved in long-term leasing agreements. While the council's position was central to the bid's rejection, its decision unquestionably represented a victory for the Tremé community.

The Tremé community's opposition to the Tivoli proposal was more intense than the opposition to the Armstrong Park Corporation's proposal. The Tivoli plan lacked the political antagonism between the mayor and city council that accompanied the Armstrong Park Corporation's proposal. This time, the mayor, council members, and the state representatives were in agreement, forcing dissenters to become more assertive. Opponents organized quickly after learning of the proposal. Although several groups made their disapproval known, the main antagonists were the TCIA and the Committee to Save Armstrong Park. While the TCIA was a long-standing organization that drew its inspiration from Hayes and Chisom, the Committee to Save Armstrong Park represented a new but higher-profile group composed of black activists from throughout the city.

The opposition to Tivoli Gardens is perhaps more easily understood in the context of the political climate of the late 1980s and early 1990s, which was characterized by a brief increase in black nationalist sentiments and a heightened interest in African identity. At the time, many blacks identified strongly with the plight of Nelson Mandela and other victims of South African apartheid. The most visible marker of this brief activist period can be found in black popular culture of the time. Politically conscious rap groups such as Public Enemy, Arrested Development, X-Clan, the Jungle Brothers, KRS-One, and A Tribe Called Quest enjoyed success, while Spike Lee's *School Daze* and *Do the Right Thing* echoed similar ideas on the big screen. During this time, African regalia and paraphernalia became popular. In the fight against Tivoli, this movement manifested itself in an effort to retain access to Congo Square.

The community activists received inspiration early in the process when the lack of private investors forced the city to seek public funding. After briefly considering a bond issue for the Tivoli project, the city decided to apply for a $36 million HUD loan. Public hearings, mandated as part of the application process, provided a forum in which members of the community could air their concerns. City council members were surprised when members of the Committee to Save Armstrong Park requested that the city withdraw its application for HUD funding. The council believed that the mayor's lengthy discussions with the TCIA, particularly Hayes and Chisom, had smoothed the way for the Tivoli project to move ahead. The vocal Committee to Save Armstrong Park saw the project as unquestionably detrimental to the Tremé neighborhood.

The TCIA and the Committee to Save Armstrong Park were not in complete disagreement over the development. Their differences involved the TCIA's perceived allegiance with the city, as evidenced by Hayes and Chisom's involvement with the Armstrong Park Committee and with the delegation that traveled to Copenhagen.[49] Hayes and Chisom were cautiously open to the Tivoli proposal contingent on the involvement of the Tremé community in running the park. On 22 March 1990, a meeting between the TCIA and the Committee to Save Armstrong Park was called to settle their disagreements. The groups emerged from the meeting united in the cause of defeating the Tivoli Park concept. As a public show of their resolve, they staged a march on City Hall on the first day of the annual Jazz and Heritage Festival.[50] Basically, the groups were calling for greater involvement in the final product. Activist Carl Galmon said, "We want to be on the front-end of developing, and later managing the park. There aren't any tourist attractions in the African American community. The jobs they are offering us involve cutting grass, picking up trash and working as a cashier in a hamburger chain, and that's not what we want." Jim Hayes, who had a longer history as a Tremé activist than Galmon, linked his concerns with the surrounding residential neighborhood, "There has to be a plan to revitalize outside the fence, we must be painting, putting roofs on and developing the community so that when tourists come, they will come to the park and at the same time, outside the fence we must have our businesses, restaurants and mom-and-pop stores — basically so we can be self-sufficient."[51]

As the spring grew into summer, there was still no word from HUD about financing. Mayor Barthelemy was becoming more pessimistic about the plan's prospects for success, fearing that Tivoli might pull out of the project. The Tivoli Armstrong Park concept began to die in the summer of 1990. It is unclear whether the project's failure resulted from the persistent activism or the lack of funding.[52] In October 1990, HUD finally granted the city a $23.5 million loan to develop Armstrong Park. That amount would cover half of the Tivoli park project, with the other half to be raised privately. With little prospect of the money being raised, both Barthelemy and Tivoli officials became disenchanted with the project. With this money in the city's pocket, however, Barthelemy continued to search for amusement-style projects for Armstrong Park well into 1991.[53] The failure of the Tivoli proposal ended Phase II efforts to privatize Armstrong Park. Another Tremé development project, however, typified city and business leaders' aspirations for the development potential of Armstrong Park and Tremé activists' concerns about potential community disruptions.

In 1991, the State of Louisiana passed legislation allowing riverboat gambling. The following year, Governor Edwin Edwards signed a bill providing for a single land-based casino in New Orleans. The casino, operated by Harrah's Jazz, was scheduled to open in the spring of 1996. Until the completion of the permanent casino's facility at the foot of Canal Street, the state decided that Municipal Auditorium would be refitted to operate for eighteen months as a temporary casino.[54]

The announcement of another large-scale development project for Armstrong Park raised familiar questions from equally familiar community activists, among them Hayes, Chisom, Randy Mitchell, and St. Mark's United Methodist Church. In addition to questions about preventing rising rents and displacement and concerns about access to Armstrong Park, critics also asked whether the casino developers would provide jobs for Tremé residents and if there were any plans to invest in Tremé beyond the improvement of the auditorium.[55]

The Tremé community won several concessions from the City of New Orleans and Harrah's Jazz. Harrah's was required to provide skilled job training for workers from Tremé and to create a Casino Relations Board to meet with concerned members of the Tremé community. In November 1994, a $41 million renovation of Municipal Auditorium began, and the casino opened on 1 May 1995, with some Tremé residents having worked on the construction project. In addition, in partnership with the Greater Tremé Consortium, a nonprofit community development organization, Harrah's established a scholarship program for students in Tremé area high schools. The temporary casino also provided lighting and landscape improvements for Armstrong Park.[56]

Any thoughts that the temporary casino would serve as an economic engine for the neighborhood were dashed when the casino garnered only one-third of its projected earnings in its first month of operation. Five months later, Harrah's closed the temporary casino, halted construction on the permanent casino, and filed for bankruptcy.[57]

CONCLUSION

The 1970s were dynamic years for urban New Orleans. Some of the city's changes were tied to political and economic developments at the national level. The Civil Rights Act of 1964 and the Voting Rights Act of 1965 had increased political participation at the same time that interstate highway construction carried whites out of New Orleans to suburban Jefferson and St. Tammany Parishes. The large-scale, federally administered programs that produced those interstates and cleared slums gave way to locally administered programs that encouraged private enterprise and community development. In the city itself, political traditionalism was replaced by a philosophy advocating tourist-oriented development while monitoring growth. The creation of Louis Armstrong Park was very much a product of these trends.

The Phase I development of Armstrong Park reflected the project's dual origins in the conflict between the patrons who favored the park as a cultural center and those who favored an entertainment-oriented park. Phase I also introduced the issues of access to and exclusion from the park. The question of admission fees magnified those issues during the Phase II development process. African American New Orleanians' decadelong opposition to the privatization of Armstrong Park resulted from the displacement of Tremé residents for the assembly center/cultural center project. In addition, activists highlighted Tremé's architectural significance, the historical importance of Tremé and Congo Square as the locus of New Orleans Creole society, and the music and parading traditions associated with Tremé-area societies and organizations.

CHAPTER SIX

National Park Savior

One night in 1998, I walked into the Tremé Community Center at 900 North Villere for the first time. The building looked older than its twenty years. I had yet to uncover the center's history or the explanation for its substandard construction. I was visiting the center to attend a community meeting organized by the National Park Service (NPS) at which officials would announce that Armstrong Park had been chosen as the site for the visitor center of the recently created New Orleans Jazz National Historical Park. At the meeting, I expected to see park superintendent Rayford Harper and assistant superintendent Robin White, both of whom I had interviewed in the park's Canal Street offices several months earlier. I was surprised to find that both Harper and White had left for other national parks. Appointed in their places were Gayle Hazelwood and Margie Ortiz. Both were new to New Orleans and to traditional jazz music, but they seemed eager to guide the park's transition from temporary quarters in a Canal Place office tower to a permanent home in Armstrong Park. After I introduced myself and my project to Hazelwood, she unexpectedly offered me the opportunity to join the park as a part-time interpreter. I eagerly agreed. On 14 February 1999, I became a park ranger (GS-7), complete with hat, badge, and cordovan shoes. For the next two years, I worked for the park service, primarily writing press releases, compiling the monthly calendar, and tackling various research assignments. I also did some interpretation and spent a lot of time telling visitors about future plans for the park. My NPS employment provided me with valuable insights and knowledge about traditional New Orleans jazz and its associated traditions as well as with the chance to learn about the park service's day-to-day business and functions. Specifically, I was privy to the relationship between the park service, the local government, and various neighborhood and community organizations, including those of Tremé. In short, during my time at the park service, I effectively wrote myself into the story of Armstrong Park and Tremé.

By the late 1980s, in New Orleans and on a national level, the nature and focus of tourism-oriented urban development had changed. Local histories and cultural traditions had come to be viewed as valuable objects of study and assets for tourism-oriented development. In New Orleans, increasing tourism had been considered an economic-development objective since the early 1970s, but such efforts typically involved commercial entertainment. The city's politicians, both cultural and elected, gradually began to support initiatives geared toward cultural enrichment, education, and preservation. For Armstrong Park, this process meant developing plans similar to those long envisioned by the Tremé community and others who recognized the city's unique cultural traditions. Not until 1999, when the New Orleans Jazz National Historical Park (NOJNHP) entered into a long-term leasing agreement with the City of New Orleans, were efforts to utilize Armstrong Park in a manner consistent with traditional New Orleans culture realized.

NATIONAL PARK SERVICE

At a time when private development proposals for Armstrong Park were at a standstill, the NPS became directly involved in Armstrong Park for the first time. For a brief period in the early 1980s, Jean Laffite National Historical Park and Preserve (JELA) leased and occupied a section of Armstrong Park's jazz complex. JELA is a multiunit park created in 1978 to preserve South Louisiana's unique cultural and natural landscapes. The park's units include the French Quarter, the Chalmette Battlefield, the Barataria (swamp) preserve, and several rural cultural units.[1] In 1987, a cooperative agreement between JELA and the City of New Orleans outlined a proposal to develop the "exterior area and the Jazz Complex in Armstrong Park" as a site dedicated to the preservation and interpretation of African American and New Orleans music and culture. Under the agreement, the Committee to Save Armstrong Park would represent the Tremé community and would serve as an advisory board to review projects and programming.[2] According to a draft of the agreement, the arrangement would expire five years from the signing date and could be terminated by either party on sixty days notice or if not renewed annually. The agreement was either never signed or immediately terminated. Nevertheless, the negotiation process marked the first time that African American culture was seriously considered as a context for Armstrong Park in a noncommercial, noncommodified manner. After the NPS's first foray into Armstrong Park failed, the development focus changed to the Tivoli plan.

At about the time that the Armstrong Tivoli Park proposal failed in 1990, JELA's mission was publicly called into question as both too diverse and not diverse enough. The *New Orleans Times-Picayune* editorial page often served as a forum for the exchange of views. On 26 March 1990, columnist Bruce Eggler lamented the "identity problem" faced by JELA, Louisiana's only national park.[3] The park's mandate of preserving and interpreting examples of the natural and historical resources of the Mississippi River Delta region had, according to Eggler, created a situation where the proliferation of subunits made JELA difficult to conceptualize. At the same time, observers called for JELA to make African American culture part of its interpretive mission. Ulysses S. Ricard Jr., assistant archivist for the Amistad Research Center at Tulane University, supported this view by noting that JELA lacked a site dedicated to the experience of African Americans in Louisiana.[4] The Park Service, he claimed, had already opened or planned cultural centers in southern Louisiana dedicated to Cajun, Native American, Isleño, and European immigrant cultures.[5]

During the same period, several other culturally oriented plans for Armstrong Park resurfaced. In an article addressing complaints about music in the French Quarter, Michael Smith, director of the New Orleans Urban Folklife Society, suggested moving "objectionable" street performances to Armstrong Park, where "such problems would be considered a blessing, and the community in Tremé could receive a greater and more direct benefit."[6] Smith also developed his ideas for Armstrong Park into a formal plan for a city park dedicated to "New Orleans Music and Cultural Heritage."[7] The potential economic windfall for the Tremé community was again noted. Although not a unique concept, Smith's proposal was one of the first and best conceived by a person outside of the local community. In the following years, several additional projects involving jazz were initiated, with a few securing substantial funding.

One idea, proposed by the Downtown Development District, advocated the creation of a linear jazz park featuring a walking path and markers along the Rampart and Basin neutral grounds. Around the same time, the state legislature considered the creation of the Louisiana Jazz Commission to commemorate jazz music and begin the process of creating a jazz hall of fame. The City of New Orleans's Music and Entertainment Commission oversaw the creation of the Black Music Hall of Fame, honoring musical contributions from across the African diaspora.[8] And the New Orleans Jazz and Heritage Foundation began plans for Buddy Bolden Place, a multipurpose entertainment complex located along the riverfront. The Black Music Hall of Fame and the Jazz and Heritage Foundation projects secured grants of $500,000 and $1 million, respectively, but only the NPS project ultimately survived. All of these ideas were either eclipsed by or incorporated into the plans for a national park dedicated to jazz.

The impetus for creating urban and cultural parks such as JELA and NOJNHP came from a 1972 symposium organized to celebrate the NPS centennial. The National Park Centennial Committee also requested that the Conservation Foundation, a not-for-profit environmental organization, assess the issues and problems facing the Park Service at that time and identify possible future issues. The project enlisted the expertise of dozens of individuals from a wide range of professions and disciplines organized into task forces charged with addressing what were deemed common points of Park Service interest. The Urban Needs and Education and Culture task forces were particularly relevant for New Orleans culture. At the project's conclusion, the Conservation Foundation offered four summary recommendations and seventeen special recommendations intended to guide future NPS policy. Each recommendation provided specific insight into the changes that the National Park Service would undergo, leading to the creation of parks similar to NOJNHP.[9]

The report recommended that U.S. cities develop public transportation linkages between urban areas and parks; promote minority park use through outreach programs; hire minorities as park rangers and NPS professionals; structure interpretive programs to reflect America's cultural diversity; develop park experiences that differed from traditional urban and suburban recreation programs; and conduct sociological research to determine how better to accommodate urban residents.[10]

Under the heading "Historical and Cultural Mission," the report's authors reasoned that in an underfunded system, the historical/cultural branch of the park service had suffered at the expense of preservation and recreation parks (including the southwestern archaeological sites). According to the authors, however, "the park system's environmental mission should not be diluted or submerged," so they recommended "as a first step, Congressional consideration of a 'National Park Historic and Cultural Coordination Act,' which would call for program planning and staff inputs of the National Park Service's historical and cultural operations from such qualified sources as the Smithsonian Institution, the National Endowment of the Arts and Humanities, and state and ethnic historical societies."[11]

The park service suggested Wolf Trap Farm, the first national park for contemporary cultural and performing arts (cited as valid and unique but not necessarily a concept that needed repeating), as an example of a park where outside arts and cultural entities could be of assistance in implementing a park's mission.[12] Although the recommended legislation never appeared, in 1980 the Park Service added to its ranks the Boston African American National Historical

Site, the Women's Rights National Historical Park, and the Martin Luther King Jr. National Historic Site. These parks are significant because they acknowledge the social and cultural significance of minority populations and their struggle for equality in the United States.[13]

In 1994, the year NOJNHP was created, the NPS underwent a congressionally mandated revision of its thematic framework to insure that "the full diversity of American history and prehistory is expressed in the National Park Service's identification and interpretation of historic properties." The social movements of the 1960s and 1970s inspired these revisions, whose goals included the expansion of interpretive programs to encompass a broader American history and an evaluation of resources to determine their suitability for addition to the National Park System or for inclusion on the list of National Historic Landmarks or the National Register of Historic Places.[14]

The revised NPS framework consisted of eight themes: the Peopling of Places; Creating Social Institutions and Movements; Expressing Cultural Values; Shaping the Political Landscape; Expanding Science and Technology; Transforming the Environment; and the Changing Role of the United States in the World Community. The themes were linked by what the NPS called the "historic building blocks" of people, time, and place. While the "people" and "time" building blocks are indeed important, the conceptualization of "place" was novel and potentially useful to the NPS: "It recognizes that region, community, and other dimensions of place are relevant. This framework acknowledges the richness of local and regional experiences and recognizes difference in place — particularly regional difference — as an important factor in a fuller understanding of both the origins of national change and the impact of national trends and events. Because place is the concrete context in which our history unfolds, a richer reconstruction of the past must include local and regional experience to help build appreciation for our national experience."[15]

In rewriting its theoretical framework, the NPS made a strong commitment toward a more socially and culturally progressive park system focused on geography. In 1996, the Park Service followed up with an equally strong commitment to social science research that was articulated in "Usable Knowledge: A Plan for Furthering Social Science and the National Parks." The NPS now sought to "conduct and promote state of the art social science related to the mission of the National Park Service, and deliver usable knowledge to the National Park Service managers and the public."[16] The plan offered several recommendations for achieving these objectives, including the establishment of a social science office in Washington, the use of special initiatives and research competitions to increase the number of social scientists working with the Park Service, and the incorporation of social science research into restructured university partnerships. The recommendations have largely been implemented, first at the national level and subsequently at the regional and park levels. Geography and economics are explicitly stated as vital and underrepresented fields among available researchers.[17]

The idea that jazz music was worthy of preservation — the concept that provided the basis for the New Orleans Jazz National Historical Park — had its roots in a 1987 Senate Concurrent Resolution, sponsored by Michigan representative John Conyers, that described jazz as "a rare and valuable natural resource to which we should devote our attention, support and resources to make certain it is preserved, understood and promulgated."[18] Although NOJNHP seems to have originated independently of the Conyers resolution, he framed jazz music in a language that rendered it worthy of NPS attention. NOJNHP was specifically created in a 1990 bill sponsored by one of Louisiana's U.S. senators, J. Bennett Johnston, chair of the Senate Appropriations Subcommittee for the Department of the Interior, that authorized a suitability and feasibility study for the creation of a unit of the National Park Service to interpret and commemorate New Orleans jazz. According to Johnston, the idea for the park

> started really actually on my back porch. My son Hunter and I were out there listening to Harry Connick, Jr. and Wynton Marsalis one evening, sipping a little sarsaparilla talking about New Orleans jazz. And the idea actually came to Hunter that "Dad, we ought to have a jazz park in New Orleans," and the lightbulb went on. And it was such an immediate obviously successful idea that I then called up [Louisiana member of Congress] Lindy [Boggs] the next day, and you know how Lindy is, anything for this city, anything for jazz. Immediately the lightbulb went on in her head as well. We began to realize the need for interpretation of New Orleans jazz, the possibilities of it; interpretation, education, or preserving the history of it.[19]

Following the authorizing legislation, the first step in the park creation process was the establishment of a citizens' committee, the Preservation of Jazz Advisory Commission. The commission's duties included advising the secretary of the U.S. Department of the Interior in preparing a suitability/feasibility study for the proposed park. The legislation required that the commission be composed of people recognized as experts on various aspects of jazz and the history and culture of Louisiana and New Orleans. Of the fifteen commissioners appointed, one was selected by the mayor, seven had doctoral degrees, one was a former member of Congress, and another was a lawyer. The Tremé community, too, was written into the feasibility study process. One member of the commission was required to be a resident of the neighborhood, and one of the commission's three public hearings was to be held in the neighborhood.[20]

Although Tremé is historically important to jazz, the neighborhood has not necessarily had any greater role in the development of or in supporting the music than have other areas. The presence of a Tremé representative on the advisory committee directly reflected neighborhood leaders' vocal activism. In fact, the composition of the advisory commission was the first park-related issue raised by Tremé's black activists.

Early in the park-planning process, Randy Mitchell, representing the Committee to Save Armstrong Park, argued that Congo Square was important in the origins of jazz and thus that representatives of Tremé merited inclusion. At one public hearing, Mitchell cautioned, "There is a tremendous amount of merit to what you are trying to do, but unless you represent our interests you are doomed to the same failure as Tivoli Gardens."[21] In Mitchell's view, Tremé's representative on the commission, Adolph Bynum, an entrepreneur and historic home renovator who had been chosen by the secretary of the interior, lacked the credentials to represent the neighborhood. Though he resided in Tremé, Bynum was seen by Mitchell and other locals as an upper-class gentrifier not attached to any of the traditions related to NOJNHP.

The public meetings held across the city as part of the planning process served as a good indicator of residents' divisions on the question of who should be in charge of telling the story of jazz as a cultural resource. Most citizens who spoke at these meetings were generally supportive of the NPS concept and tended to favor locating the park within Armstrong Park. Some who opposed the idea did so for reasons that were strongly related to race. For example, white jazz "expert" Al Rose bashed the project as intellectually unsound because it failed to define jazz (or, more accurately, failed to adhere to his definition). Rose dismissed what he called the "myth of jazz's African origins," contending that Italians "have a substantial history in the development of Jazz."[22] A fair number of blacks were unhappy with what they perceived as impending white control of a black resource. These speakers offered arguments that at times seemed reasonable but at other times seemed fanciful or revisionist. At the core of their thinking, however, lay the irreparable harm suffered by the Tremé community throughout the twentieth century.

In the fall of 1992, after more than a year of public meetings and research, the commission reported to Congress that a unit of JELA should be created with the goal of supporting local jazz education programs and working to preserve sites important to jazz. The report suggested that the unit have a visitor center in Armstrong Park.

On 31 October 1994, satisfied with the findings of the resource/feasibility study and the commission's recommendations, Congress passed Public Law 103-433, which established the New Orleans Jazz National Historical Park. According to the bill, the park was created "in furtherance of the need to recognize the value and importance of jazz, . . . to preserve the origins, early history, development and progression of jazz; provide visitors with opportunities to experience the sights, sounds and places where jazz evolved; and implement innovative ways of establishing jazz educational partnerships that will help ensure that jazz continues as a vital element of the culture of New Orleans and our nation."[23]

The formal creation of NOJNHP represented the beginning of a long process that involved the development of a general management plan/environmental impact statement. The management plan presented three alternative forms for the park: no action; an NPS personal service approach, to be headquartered at the U.S. Mint on Esplanade Avenue; and a partnership emphasis, to be headquartered at Armstrong Park.[24] The management plan presented the details of each alternative, including the projected cost, impacts, and consequences of each choice. To inform this decision and to assist the park in its future mission, the park's legislation created the New Orleans Jazz Commission, a holdover concept from the earlier advisory commission. As part of the process of preparing the draft management plan, the NPS held twelve public meetings and produced four newsletters in 1996 and 1997.

While the NPS was conducting public meetings, the City of New Orleans was following its own policies. Local government perceived the establishment of NOJNHP as a source of city pride and an excellent opportunity to sustain the cultural traditions that made the city a tourist destination. To Mayor Marc Morial, son of former mayor Ernest N. "Dutch" Morial, NOJNHP represented a political accomplishment and a chance to unload the burden of operating Armstrong Park, Municipal Auditorium, and the Mahalia Jackson Theater for the Performing Arts. Morial requested that the City Planning Commission and Capital Projects Department draft a "proposed uses" plan for the New Orleans Jazz National Historical Park in Armstrong Park. The slick document called for a grand renovation of the Municipal Auditorium and the Theater for the Performing Arts, an overhaul of the park's physical landscape, and the addition of an amphitheater, ideas that recalled the glitzy 1980s plans in scale and cost.[25] However, Johnston announced his impending retirement, making uncertain the prospects for further funding of NOJNHP. Furthermore, threats to reduce the number of national parks were coming from the new Republican-controlled Congress.[26]

Morial and other city officials undertook these efforts without consulting with the NPS. According to Jack Stewart, a New Orleans musician, jazz historian, and preservationist, Johnston "was supposed to funnel $50 million through the Park Service as a gift to the city, and the Park Service was supposed to be the pass-through agency for this money. Finally, the $50 million came down to $5 million, down to $3.5 million, and $3.5 million to a visitor center. I remember the director of the planning commission asking, 'Can we at least do a study?' The Park Service said, 'We don't need a study. We know what we want to do.'"[27]

In 1998, NOJNHP unveiled its own development plans in accordance with the legislative mandate for a draft management plan. Officials chose the partnership option, endorsing a concept whereby NOJNHP would partner with other public and private entities to fulfill its mission. The proposal also included an emphasis on jazz education and, most important, on preserving the historical and cultural resources related to jazz and locating a visitor and interpretive center in Armstrong Park. In August 1999, NOJNHP entered into a long-term leasing agreement with the City of New Orleans to occupy the jazz complex and adjacent green space for its visitor center.[28] The decision to locate NOJNHP in Armstrong Park progressed in much the same manner, or with the same logic, as the 1972 decision to locate the Louis Armstrong Memorial in the unfinished cultural center. In the earlier case, forty years of failed civic center and cultural center plans left a void in the landscape and skepticism that the city's leadership could efficiently oversee the urban development. Likewise, the failure to complete the Phase II development of Armstrong Park made NOJNHP the favored candidate for developing this area.

Although many citizens were pleased with plans to do something with Armstrong Park and expressed hope that NOJNHP would improve the area's image, not everyone approved of the development plan. Some members of the public transferred their long-standing concerns regarding the area's safety directly to the national park proposition. Some objections about the proposed location's suitability bordered on racist. The final version of the management plan contained many skeptical and/or negative comments about Armstrong Park/Tremé.

According to one "jazz photographer/writer," "Louis Armstrong Park and the entire area north of Bourbon Street is not safe. We have friends who have been mugged there, and we did not feel safe when visiting the park in the daytime. We did not stay long. This issue is not well addressed in your document. What can be done to improve safety in that neighborhood?" Commented another person, "The success of this proposal depends on improving the image of the Armstrong Park neighborhood for tourists (as well as many residents). The neighborhood must be more secure, and the visitor must feel safe to visit the Park." More harshly, someone else wrote,

> The goals of the park will never be reached if its primary location is Armstrong Park for the following reasons.
>
> 1) Due to its controversial history, there may never be an agreement reached between neighborhood leaders and government on its use.
>
> 2) The question of safety in the park will be difficult to address. Since the shooting death of a tourist at mid day in the late 1980s, all ground level tourist handlers tell them *not* to go in the park.

Organizations also weighed in, in some cases more diplomatically. Wrote the Vieux Carré Property Owners, Residents, and Associates, "The growth and development of the jazz park will probably result in welcome increases in security and safety in the area simply because of increased numbers of visitors. In addition, though, it is important to include security personnel among the park's anticipated professional staff."[29]

It is difficult objectively to discern the impact of crime or its perception on the selection of Armstrong Park as the site of NOJNHP. The park's explicitly secured landscape, defined by its fenced perimeter, the limited hours of access, and the location of a police substation there have not been enough to counter its dangerous reputation. However, with few exceptions, violent crime does not really occur in Armstrong Park.[30] Still, the park's reputation for crime is at least partly responsible for its relative lack of patrons. The perception of crime may have been greater than the actual threat. A 1995 study by the College of Urban and Public Affairs at the University of New Orleans found that the typical correlation between crime and income does not apply to Tremé: police statistics reveal that Tremé's crime rate in early 1990s was lower than that of other parts of the city. The report concludes that Tremé's isolation from the surrounding area reduces criminal activity. On three sides, Tremé is bounded by "hard edges" — that is, borders that are "not easily passable, often due to physical design." Claiborne Avenue/Interstate 10, Rampart Street, and Armstrong Park seal off the neighborhood, leaving Esplanade as the only thoroughfare in and out of Tremé. These hard edges buffer the neighborhood from surrounding high-crime areas, particularly the Iberville and Lafitte housing projects.[31]

Regardless of Tremé's actual crime rate, potential visitors perceive the area as dangerous. Such perceptions are generated in part in the French Quarter, where visitors have long been warned not to venture beyond Bourbon Street and certainly not "behind the Quarter." Because the park's headquarters were not located in Armstrong Park, management was concerned about vandalism of the NOJNHP complex's buildings. The park's security concerns highlight the problem of having vacant buildings in an unregulated space and to a certain extent support the logic of retaining the park's fence. The park's managers were also concerned with the public's perception of Armstrong Park in terms of both aesthetics and safety. Park rangers patrolled Armstrong Park in pairs during the middle of the day and collected data on the number of visitors. Rangers also queried visitors about their impressions of the park.[32] Most visitors thought that the park seemed underutilized and did not understand why. Even though the lagoons were not pristine and walkways had cracks, the park had charms that reflective individuals could appreciate.

Armstrong Park's design also presented problems. The factors that influence visitor perceptions of public safety also link directly to park aesthetics — people feel safer in developed parks with few trees and long sight lines. It is ironic that removing vegetation increases visibility and makes people feel safer yet potentially reduces a park's aesthetic qualities.[33] In Armstrong Park, developers had created landscaped berms to contrast with the region's naturally flat topography. Furthermore, the park is filled with large buildings and dense foliage, providing additional points of visitor uncertainty; someone could be lurking close by but out of sight. Finally, although the fence limits access, it also prevents people from fleeing should a threat appear. Park management and staff considered public safety an important secondary issue.

The 1998 leasing agreement with the city seemed to clear the way for NOJNHP to create a visitor center in Armstrong Park, although two problems remained to be resolved. First, funding had to be obtained. Johnston eventually obtained $3.1 million, but that amount was less than officials needed to open a visitor center, even by adapting existing buildings. Moreover, Formosan termites had already done considerable damage to the jazz complex. Planners realized that treating for termites, repairing the damage, and then renovating the building would be a long-term project.[34] Extending that timetable was Park Service/ federal government policy, which required a lengthy bidding process to select contractors. At the end of the millennium, the prospect that NOJNHP would move to Armstrong Park still seemed remote.

From 1994 to 2000, the Park Service carried out its mission from its offices in the Canal Place tower at the foot of Canal Street. The park's nontraditional nature permitted its operation without a visitor center, although some difficulties arose. Jazz education took place in schools, interviews of aging musicians occurred in their homes, and live performances were scheduled across the city. In the summer of 2000, however, the NOJNHP visitor's center moved into temporary facilities in the French Quarter, making the center accessible to one of the country's largest tourist populations. There, regularly scheduled performances and lectures could make use of the park's growing collection of audio, visual, and multimedia information on traditional New Orleans jazz. With its interpretive, educational, and preservationist missions accomplished and the Armstrong Park's construction in the hands of the National Park Service's Southeast Regional Offices in Atlanta, NOJNHP was on the way to becoming a part of the national park system. Still unresolved, however, was the issue of the park's relationship with the Tremé community.

From the outset, many Tremé activists supported plans to create NOJNHP and advocated its location in Armstrong Park. However, community support was neither unconditional nor uncomplicated. Park service personnel contend that since the creation of NOJNHP, certain Tremé activists have tried to exact preferential treatment from the National Park Service. Both Harper, NOJNHP's first superintendent, and his assistant, White, faced pressure from both Uptown and Downtown community groups for what amounted to economic assistance.[35]

For several years, plans to develop Armstrong Park were linked with efforts to develop the community, including calls for improved housing, increasing the level of owner occupancy, halting gentrification and displacement, and providing employment opportunities. Yet neither the park's resource study nor the general management plan acknowledged the economic disparity and politically contentious debates that exist in Tremé.[36] This shortsightedness raises the question of whether the NPS bears responsibility only for the park's official mission or whether the Park Service has a greater social responsibility for the surrounding area. If the National Park Service is going to be responsible for the protection of cultural resources, it also follows that it needs to deal with the pragmatic dimensions of culture, including place and even poverty. However, it seems unlikely that the park will explicitly or outwardly involve itself in local development, meaning that the community must consider how the park can address social and economic concerns.

Along with Mitchell, Tremé activist Jerome Smith, who holds a seat on the New Orleans Jazz Commission and serves as director of the Tremé Community Center, has stood at the forefront of many community protests targeting

Armstrong Park. In the past, Smith has expressed outrage over several issues, most notably NOJNHP's attempt to establish a jazz education program at Tremé's Craig Elementary School without his permission. At one point Smith requested that NOJNHP divert part of the money earmarked for the construction of its visitor center toward funding a full-time music teacher at the same school. But, argued Hazelwood, "It is not our responsibility or role to right the wrongs that have been done to the Tremé neighborhood." In her opinion, NOJNHP is not in the position to demand jobs for Tremé residents, act as a granting agency for Tremé programs, or serve as the neighborhood's economic engine: "The park's decisions should not be made because of perceived economic advantages but on the merit of the resources being protected." More appropriately, NOJNHP should be seen as "the hub of the wheel," providing tangential or spin-off advantages for the community.[37]

CONCLUSION

The damages done to Tremé in the 1960s can never be repaired, but the NPS's presence in Armstrong Park brought an end to the proposed uses for Armstrong Park that excluded Tremé residents or betrayed their cultural past. That it has taken a federal presence to bring stability to Armstrong Park is ironic, given the U.S. government's past role in disrupting the community. While the community continues to monitor the activities at Armstrong Park, often using older methods of protest, its efforts can now be directed in different ways.

Following the era of privatization, the Tremé community's call for constructive uses of Armstrong Park that were consistent with the cultural traditions of the neighborhood began to resonate with the people of Greater New Orleans. At the same time, activists called for changes in JELA's focus. On a national level, the Park Service increasingly directed its attention to urban and minority populations, in part by designating parks that were more representative of America's diverse cultural and historical resources. The intersection of those movements led to the creation of New Orleans Jazz National Historical Park. In addition to recognizing jazz music, a multiethnic art form rooted in the African American experience, NOJNHP was also charged with recognizing New Orleans's African American parading traditions. The decision to locate the NOJNHP visitor center in Armstrong Park transformed the park from a public space scheduled for privatization to a liminal space with the potential to satisfy, at least partially, the desires of both the Tremé community and the city.

The creation of NOJNHP is relevant beyond Armstrong Park and Tremé.

The process was explicitly spatial, emphasizing parade routes and the location of important jazz-related sites and structures. The geographical nature of the process was in line with the Park Service's goal of becoming more sensitive to place. Furthermore, in filling the New Orleans Jazz Commission and Advisory Board with politically influential people knowledgeable about the cultural landscape, the NPS increased the scale of both NOJNHP and Armstrong Park, thereby making the issue relevant to people beyond the local community.

CHAPTER SEVEN

Saving Black Tremé

On 23 November 2003, I found myself at a second-line parade in Downtown New Orleans. This is not the Downtown referred to in previous chapters — the Fifth, Sixth, and Seventh Wards — but the Ninth Ward, which is way Downtown. It was the first Ninth Ward second-line parade in which I had participated during the half dozen years I had followed the tradition.[1] On that Sunday afternoon, I was in the Ninth Ward because a week earlier I had received a route sheet advertising this parade, and what I saw piqued my curiosity.[2] The parade was celebrating the fifth anniversary of Lady Nine Times, the female auxiliary of the Nine Times Social and Pleasure Club. The parade was to start at Magee's bar on Louisa Street in the Ninth Ward and wind through the Desire neighborhood. The location of the parade might have led me to skip it, but when I read the names of the members of the royal court, I decided to attend. Every male member of the court was a member of the Bynum family, including the king, Adolph Bynum. The Nine Times club was honoring the Bynums because of their role as model community members.[3]

Bynum, the owner of a pharmacy on Piety Street and St. Claude Avenue, is an African American resident of Tremé often noted for renovating historical properties in the neighborhood. He is also lauded for working to transform the neighborhood into a cleaner and safer place. In the early 1980s, Bynum purchased and renovated two properties on St. Claude, and he has since acquired several others. He and his wife, Naydja, have also constructed a cottage in Tremé modeled on a nineteenth-century Creole design. Bynum's renovation and neighborhood improvement efforts are the basis for his public persona; he sits on organization boards and committees and is the frequent subject of magazine articles.[4]

If the Adolph Bynum being honored in the parade was the same person who lived in Tremé, I could think of no greater situational irony. This successful family was participating in a largely working-class tradition, but that alone is not ironic. Class lines do not strictly regulate participation in New Orleans performance traditions. But Bynum's second Tremé persona—not simply historic renovator but also gentrifier—draws the ire of Tremé neighborhood activists because he is leading a movement whose consequences involve removing affordable housing stock beyond the means of the neighborhood's working-class and poor African American residents. In addition, this movement also threatens Tremé's long-standing musical and parading traditions, which are based in part on neighborhood affiliation and localized performance.

Whether viewed as a saint or a villain, Bynum embodies a movement to renovate or preserve historic housing in Tremé and other neighborhoods. Bynum is significant because although he has been renovating houses in Tremé for twenty years, he represents the changing face of gentrification, altering the black-white binary that defined the gentrification discourse developed almost forty years ago. In addition to individual gentrifiers such as the Bynums, Tremé is also affected by what might be considered the gentrifying local state—that is, a government actively changing neighborhood dynamics by influencing housing politics, policy, and policing activities. All these factors converged outside the boundaries of Armstrong Park in the 1990s to produce a unique housing struggle. However, the events transpiring outside the park were not necessarily separate from the events that influenced the park.

The term *gentrification* was coined in the decades following World War II to describe a housing process occurring in large North American and European cities wherein middle-class residents purchased and fixed up homes in decaying inner cities. The process ran counter to the more predominant exodus from cities to suburbs under way at the same time. Gentrification has subsequently been examined from many perspectives, including gentrifiers' motivations and the process's impact on longtime residents of an area. Until the 1980s, it was believed that gentrification was either economic (that is, based on the exploitation of the rent gap and tied to changing financing structures and housing markets) or cultural (that is, a process wherein individuals identify with and derive meaning from aestheticized architecture or some other aspect of urban living).[5] Gentrification has subsequently proven to be more complex and nuanced. Nevertheless, there is widespread agreement, including in Tremé, that the process negatively affects a neighborhood's long-standing residents by either changing the area's character or increasing property values so that these residents are displaced from their homes or unable to find affordable housing. Because residential displacement differentially impacts poor and minority populations, the terms *gentrification* and *gentrifier* have taken on pejorative connotations, leading those engaged in the activity to reject those labels and to see themselves as renovators of deteriorating properties, engaged in historic preservation. Alternately, those who champion the poor and those who suffer from gentrification see gentrifiers as profit-driven outsiders.

In New Orleans, the Faubourg Marigny is often cited as the city's first gentrified neighborhood.[6] Bernard Marigny created the suburb just downriver of the Vieux Carré shortly before Claude Tremé did the same to the rear. Not surprisingly, the Marigny has a history and ethnic composition similar to those of other Downtown neighborhoods — that is, it has Creole origins and was integrated and multiethnic. By the second half of the twentieth century, when New Orleans began experiencing white flight, the Marigny saw a substantial influx of poorer black residents, accompanied by increasing landlord neglect. This situation produced the rent gap considered necessary for gentrification. In the 1970s, a group of gay men and others began moving into the part of the Marigny adjacent to the French Quarter. Many in this group, which became the Marigny's first wave of gentrifiers, were associated with the newly created University of New Orleans (originally Louisiana State University at New Orleans). They chose the neighborhood because it was a conveniently located alternative to the pricier French Quarter. Those early arrivals began speculating in real estate and touting a historic preservation ethos. At present, the Marigny is New Orleans's most gentrified neighborhood. Renovators and speculators looking for Downtown options must seek opportunities in other neighborhoods.

The Marigny's transition from a place of deteriorating housing stock to a gentrified middle-class neighborhood leads to the question of why Tremé did not share in that experience. After all, Faubourg Tremé is similar to the Marigny in architecture, multiethnic social history, and proximity to the French Quarter. Larry Knopp, whose research reconstructed the Marigny's transformation from a working-class neighborhood into a middle-class gay neighborhood in the 1960s and 1970s, speculates that Tremé possessed too many disincentives to gentrify at the same time and on the scale of the Marigny.[7]

Tremé's material disincentives in the late 1960s and 1970s included the presence of U.S. Interstate 10, an uncertain cultural center/Armstrong Park project, and the neighborhood's proximity to the Iberville and Lafitte public housing projects. The specific effect of distressed public housing on urban development and well-being is difficult to quantify. In most cities, including New Orleans, the business community and local government see public housing as an obstacle to development.[8] It is not difficult to believe that white gays feared living near large numbers of poor blacks. Social reluctance thus slowed the entrance of gays into the neighborhood. Knopp notes that the Marigny "was a predominantly white neighborhood and was much more removed from the housing projects. A vivid bi-racial and multi-cultural social history made it easy for whites to settle there without feeling that they were applying racist standards to their decisions."[9] Tremé activists may have played an even more important role in discouraging gentrification. According to Knopp, Tremé residents "fought, they fought, they fought! The blacks [of Tremé] resisted change because of the race situation."[10]

It is hard to imagine exactly how Tremé activists could have resisted individual efforts to purchase and renovate homes in the area. But given Tremé's history of activism, it is possible that during the 1970s and 1980s, community leaders may have been inhospitable to organized preservation efforts. Such was certainly the case in the 1990s, when the Preservation Resource Center was not actively involved in the neighborhood because of resident hostility. From the beginning of Tremé's post-civil-rights activism, the housing welfare of long-standing community residents was a primary concern, and it remained so through the Armstrong Park and Harrah's Casino debates.

Despite protests by some Tremé residents, the neighborhood is changing. Tremé's contemporary housing landscape illustrates that renovation efforts in Tremé are concentrated in the neighborhood's eastern section, in the vicinity of St. Augustine Church. In those blocks, incomes are higher, real estate is more valuable, and there are more white residents. There are no solid indicators that explain why that area gentrified first. The general consensus is that those blocks have always been whiter. Common sense, conversely, suggests that those areas are farther from the neighborhood's perceived negative amenities and closer to the French Quarter and Esplanade Avenue, the Downtown equivalent of St. Charles Avenue. There is also no clear indication of when the gentrification process in Tremé began. It is possible that Bynum began Tremé's gentrification movement. He readily admits that the first properties he purchased in the neighborhood, now Tremé's gentrification core, were boarded up at the time. He eventually came to own the entire block.[11]

By the early 1990s, people were renovating houses farther away from the core area, closer to Armstrong Park and Claiborne Avenue/I-10. Urban affairs and real estate journalists and others chronicled the trend in local periodicals. A *New Orleans Times-Picayune* article from January 2000 heralded Tremé's renovation boom, quoting one renovator as saying, "Four or five years ago there were some real bargains on Esplanade, but no more. Those days are over on Esplanade, but you can see interest and renewal spilling over block-by-block into the streets off Esplanade."[12] Many of those streets are in Tremé.

Father Jerome LeDoux, a priest at St. Augustine, notes the increased presence of whites in the neighborhood and cites their relaxed behavior as evidence that Tremé is becoming more like the French Quarter: "You can walk around at eleven at night, midnight, one o'clock in the morning, you see a lone white male or female walking here. You would not have seen that fifteen years ago. They feel secure here because more are coming here. They are literally driving back the black frontier. And in a way, they would think and say 'the frontiers of crime and drug trafficking,' which is only a partial truth, but that is the mindset. You can see people walking in pairs, not looking behind them, as if to say, 'I'm at home here.' And many of them are."[13]

Several factors account for the boom in gentrified housing in Tremé. On the surface, the neighborhood's cultural history and/or the public's knowledge of that history made the neighborhood a cool and trendy place to live, especially for those involved in various aspects of New Orleans culture. Tremé also fit other locational criteria. It was affordable and close to the French Quarter. In fact, Tremé newcomers often voice the same considerations for moving there that Marigny gentrifiers listed in the 1970s.[14] For all its hipness and diversity and the strength of the national economy and housing market during the 1990s, the effects of gentrification in the area should not be overlooked. Without readily available mortgage and finance capital, it is unclear whether Tremé's housing boom would have been possible. The role of the government also should not be overlooked. Gentrification has never been solely an individual proposition, occurring at the whim of the eager investor or urban pioneer. The state has always been involved, most notably by making neighborhoods safe and investments secure, both literally and figuratively. Real estate investors require legal and financial stability, conditions that government policy can ensure. As state involvement has increased, so has gentrification. In 1966, for example, the federal government indirectly encouraged gentrification by passing the National Historic Preservation Act, adding to the federal government's commitment to preserving historically significant sites.[15] New Orleans's French Quarter was one of the act's first beneficiaries. At the time, the Quarter's integrity was threatened by a proposed riverfront bypass for Interstate 10. In fact, the act explicitly sought to protect sites threatened by land-consuming federal infrastructure projects such as urban renewal and interstate highway construction.

The act also created the National Register of Historic Places as an instrument to inventory significant sites, ordered the list's expansion, and redefined the "historic district" concept.[16] In 1966, the French Quarter became the first New Orleans neighborhood to receive national register recognition, followed by the Garden District (1971), the Lower Garden District (1972), and Faubourg Marigny (1974). Most important, the act advocated the creation of state- and local-level preservation offices, which in turn produced the 1974 Louisiana

Archaeological Treasures Act and the 1976 creation of the New Orleans Historic District Landmarks Commission (HDLC). In spirit, the state and local entities reinforced the concerns of the National Historic Preservation Act. In practice, these efforts have produced a confusing, overlapping hierarchy of preservation interests and authorities, including federal, state, and local governmental agencies; nongovernmental interests; and independent neighborhood associations. The HDLC has the most meaningful local enforcement powers, bestowing "certificates of appropriateness" on everything from new construction and demolitions to millwork and signage.

The national-level concern for preservation inspired neighborhoods to form organizations promoting a wide range of local interests, among them safety and architectural integrity. One of the best early examples was the Faubourg Marigny Improvement Association, founded in 1972 to "protect, support, and maintain Faubourg Marigny." Specifically, the group sought to "promote the physical, cultural, architectural and historical values of said section and to secure adequate enforcement of all laws of the City of New Orleans and the State of Louisiana affecting or pertaining to it."[17] One of the group's first successes in that regard was securing special zoning for the Marigny Triangle area to protect it from incompatible, out-of-character, or inappropriately scaled uses. The Marigny Improvement Association also advocated the neighborhood's addition to the local, state, and national historic registers. Residents in the Esplanade Ridge and Tremé areas also created neighborhood associations in 1972, but they did not endure. Two years later, the Preservation Resource Center (PRC), a citywide advocacy group, was formed to "promote the preservation, restoration, and revitalization of New Orleans's historic architecture and neighborhoods."[18] The group has subsequently become the city's most widely recognized preservation entity. In addition to keeping watch over the architectural landscape, the PRC offers a range of educational, outreach, and funding programs.

The PRC's core philosophy is a conviction that "preserving a city's architecture is tantamount to preserving its soul."[19] Indeed, because of the efforts of the PRC and similarly minded neighborhood groups, New Orleans's future identity will at least partially rest on its architectural distinctiveness. But architecture comprises only a part of New Orleans's identity. The city's soul is also expressed in its vibrant cultural traditions. The normalization of historic preservation and the proliferation of historic districts over the past forty years have encouraged gentrification and threatened the material foundations of New Orleans's performative culture by deterritorializing low-income African American residents. This argument fits into a more basic and generalizable debate about the integrity of long-standing communities.

The mechanism by which this deterritorialization takes place is architectural fetishism, or the elevation of architectural considerations (detailing and historical accuracy on a small scale and homogeneity and appropriate scale at the neighborhood level) over issues such as functionality and affordability. The relationship between architectural fetishism and real estate speculation should not be assumed to exist a priori. Historically, first-wave gentrifiers were not speculators, and real estate speculators were interested in properties and areas where historical architecture was not a consideration. Nevertheless, larger cities typically have speculative real estate markets geared specifically toward renovators. Both groups, however, are aided by territorially defined historic districts. Although outwardly seeking to create homogenous architectural districts, historic districts work to eliminate social and economic differences that can work against the interests of both speculators and renovators or increasingly the speculative renovator. Furthermore, historic districts make homogenization, potentially a confrontational process, easier by placing enforcement on unassailable boundary or enforcement entity.

At the local level, then, the state is directly involved in the process of gentrification through the HDLC and its oversight of historic districts. New Orleans's local government also plays a role in gentrification through its overall housing policy, presently administered by the Office of Housing and Neighborhood Development, which works to address the fundamental housing concerns (provision, safety, and so forth) that have long plagued the poorer areas of the city. In addressing those issues, however, the city may inadvertently stimulate gentrification by improving neighborhoods' overall character and thereby removing disincentives to renovation. Such is not the case for every neighborhood. It is doubtful, for example, that city-led housing improvements in the Desire or Holly Grove neighborhoods would attract a gentrifying middle class since those areas lack historic architecture, an essential component for gentrification.

The New Orleans government's approach to housing and community development issues over the past thirty years has been influenced by the fact that the city has elected black mayors and officials. The resulting political regimes formed governing coalitions that forged development policies, including housing, that supported the predominantly white business community while not appearing hostile to working-class African Americans.

New Orleans's African American mayors, from Ernest N. "Dutch" Morial to Ray Nagin, have led different types of political administrations and therefore have assembled different types of growth and development coalitions. The administrations have reflected the political and racial compositions of their respective electorates. Sidney Barthelemy won his first term (1986–90), for example, by securing a majority of New Orleans's more conservative white voters and therefore employed a more conservative governing style than did either Dutch or Marc Morial. One of the manifestations of this style was less direct governmental involvement in local housing concerns. Instead, New Orleans saw growth in nonprofit housing organizations or, in the case of public housing, task forces composed of a combination of interested parties. In theory, these organizations would use grant money to build affordable housing in designated communities, using local labor and companies when possible. Housing nonprofits were attractive options for the local government because they shifted the development concerns to communities and served as small-scale patronage mechanisms with the possibility of yielding results and silencing grassroots activists. This method of injecting money into African American communities soon proved controversial, however, when some nonprofits were more interested in lining their staff's pockets than helping provide and improve housing.

In Tremé, community-based nonprofit and religious organizations have long been a source of housing assistance and a basis for community activism. The Tremé Community Improvement Association and Tambourine and Fan are Tremé's oldest existing neighborhood organizations, but they were not always necessarily oriented toward housing. The Greater Tremé Neighborhood Consortium, whose president is Tremé Community Improvement Association cofounder James Hayes, was one of the neighborhood's first organizations explicitly dedicated to economic development and housing. The consortium, funded by several public and private entities, provided emergency home repair, owner-occupied housing rehabilitation, home-buyer counseling, and neighborhood beautification for Tremé. The consortium received significant funding from Harrah's Casino for the purpose of mitigating any detrimental effects caused by the temporary casino in Armstrong Park, one of which was the displacement of long-time Tremé residents. While the consortium and other agencies have had some measure of success, other groups have run into problems managing what amounted to small companies.

Several Tremé nonprofits created in the 1990s have been suspected of mismanaging funds. The Tremé Cultural Enrichment Corporation, which was headed by an appellate court judge and oversaw $478,000 in state funds, closed with few results and under suspicion of budgetary improprieties.[20] The most notorious of Tremé's community-based organizations was the

Armstrong Redevelopment Corporation (ARC). Created in 1992 and staffed by the Barthelemy administration, the ARC administered a $3.2 million federal special-purpose grant for housing rehabilitation in Tremé. The agency was administered by Barthelemy associate Endesha Juakali. Prior to joining the ARC, Juakali served as chair of the embattled Housing Authority of New Orleans. In its two years of operation, the ARC frivolously spent $1 million, prompting a city audit. With Barthelemy's aid, the ARC survived attacks from within the government, but in 1994, newly elected mayor Marc Morial closed the agency.[21] The ARC's closure did not put an end to the issue. The federal government launched an investigation and threatened to force the city to repay millions of misspent dollars and to transfer the remaining funds to another city.[22] Morial, however, had other plans for the money and Tremé.

Marc Morial was elected to his first of two terms in 1994. Morial presided over a growing city with a drastically reduced violent crime rate. He also fully embraced New Orleans's role as a tourist city in a globalizing world, including the recognition of culture, art, history, and architecture for the local economy. Although Barthelemy's second term coincided with the rise of the cultural economy, the younger and more charismatic Morial proved more adept at harnessing New Orleans's cultural resources for both his political benefit and the benefit of the local economy.

Gentrification in Tremé also accelerated during Morial's mayoralty, likely spurred by the city's favorable economy and reduced crime rate. Not surprisingly, the city increased its presence in the neighborhood at the same time. The Morial administration inherited a local housing situation that had shown little improvement in previous years and a housing department charged with the mismanagement of federal grant money. Morial appointed his campaign manager, Vincent Sylvain, to lead the city's housing department and formulate a plan to address the city's housing needs. Sylvain implemented what he called the Impact Neighborhood Strategy, which clustered housing activities within certain geographical areas. The city initially selected four blighted areas with development potential, including Tremé.

The city's effort to improve Tremé's housing included a plan to benefit owner-occupied homes. The city promised to renovate the interiors of approximately thirty homes owned by people with low incomes. For exteriors, the city sponsored a paint program designed to have a ripple effect on other properties. To stem the tide of gentrification and keep traditional residents in the neighborhood, the city offered special financing, down-payment assistance, purchase options, and a first-time buyers' program.[23]

The cornerstone of the city's attempt to revive Tremé was the stately Villa-Milleur mansion on Governor Nicholls Road. The city planned to use the remaining $1.8 million in ARC funds to renovate the building and open a museum. To advance the idea, Morial prompted the creation of the Tremé Historical Development Corporation. The federal investigation threatened the city's attempt to secure the ARC funds, and in the end New Orleans had to provide assurances that the money would be used properly.[24] In hopes of augmenting the available funds, the city presented a proposal to the banking community to build a museum to "benefit and recognize the Tremé community and African Americans in particular and their contributions to New Orleans, both from a cultural standpoint and an architectural standpoint."[25] The city spent $1.2 million to renovate the building and grounds, including the slave quarters. The city later purchased several adjacent residential properties, converting them into a gallery hall and exhibit space. Plans also called for a sculpture garden and the renovation of a second Creole-style structure to house a permanent Tremé museum.

During the Morial administration, the Tremé Villa became a showpiece. Within its iron fence (not unlike that of Armstrong Park), the grounds were maintained in pristine condition. The gardens remained well manicured and the exterior walls freshly painted. Inside the villa, the refinished wood floors reflected the rotating art exhibits coordinated by museum director Stephanie Jordan. The museum also hosted gala events, drawing New Orleans's African American aristocracy in gowns and luxury sedans and protected by a police department patrol car conspicuously parked on the street.

The Tremé Villa and the African American museum it housed, as well as the Tremé Historical Development Corporation, can be viewed in several ways. Some observers saw the museum as a showplace, while others saw it as more about Morial. It can also be viewed as a form of black gentrification to counter the white gentrification in Tremé — that is, as part of an attempt to establish an African American presence in Tremé before the opportunity to do so had passed. At the time of the museum's establishment, the city's residents were well aware of Tremé's history of radical Creole politics and performance traditions as well as the explosion of renovations in the area. Some New Orleanians considered the Villa the city's attempt to cash in on the trendy neighborhood. But all of these explanations are too simplistic: fully comprehending the city's actions requires an understanding of New Orleans's racialized settlement and migration patterns. Even though many members of New Orleans's black middle class live away from Downtown in such neighborhoods as New Orleans

East, Gentilly, and Algiers, many of these people, including Marc Morial, have roots in Tremé and the Seventh Ward. In a sense, the attempt to establish and maintain a black presence in Tremé is a way of coming back home and of encouraging other African Americans to do so as well.

In October 1998, also during Morial's tenure, the city council created the Tremé Historic District, which was carved out of the 250-block Esplanade Ridge Historic District created eighteen years earlier. The district includes the area bounded by North Rampart, Orleans, North Broad, and Esplanade as well as a triangular section bounded by St. Bernard and North Claiborne Avenues that was part of the original Tremé suburb but is in the Seventh Ward. Because the new historic district came out of an existing jurisdiction, no new structures came under HDLC control.

Nevertheless, the district's creation was roundly celebrated as long-overdue recognition for the historic neighborhood. Tremé area city council member Troy Carter declared, "I see this as an opportunity to set the record straight and to correct a historical error." Activist Randy Mitchell agreed, believing that black Tremé residents had been overlooked when the Esplanade Ridge district was established.[26]

Members of the Esplanade Ridge Civic Association did not welcome the creation of the new historic district, however. An association spokesman told the council that although the members of his group did not oppose the move, they were disappointed about not being included in the process and skeptical about the thoroughness of the research performed prior to the decision.[27] This position probably reflected the Esplanade Ridge Civic Association's concerns about losing influence.

Such disputes illuminate the symbolic power of historic districts. The creation of the Tremé Historic District legitimized issues — many of which were unrelated to historic structures — long advocated by the Tremé community. The designation also validated the assertion that Tremé extends beyond Claiborne Avenue. Unlike the more affluent Esplanade Ridge community, the idea of Tremé benefits from the additional tracts of Sixth Ward housing and gains territorial legitimacy where political and economic authority is fleeting. In short, Tremé advocates welcomed the formation of the district because it confirmed their view that their neighborhood was special, a point confirmed by the fact that the council session was interrupted briefly by the Tremé brass band. However, questions remain about the extent to which the HDLC cares about the cultural and historical uniqueness that Tremé residents were celebrating at the council meeting and about how the existence of the new district could exacerbate gentrification.

Longtime Tremé residents and their activist advocates are aware of the gentrification process and its consequences. While some research suggests that newcomers do not always have a significant negative impact on long-term residents, most studies find the process detrimental because of residential dislocation and alienation.[28] Analyses of displacement often rely on census data to document neighborhood transition. Ethnographic evidence, however, provides a more personal look into gentrification. Ebony Bolding has recently described her family's displacement from a quiet neighborhood on North Dorgenois to Dumaine Street (both of which are in Tremé) after the landlord sold the house. Bolding interviewed the man who purchased her family's home and others, both white and black, who have moved into the neighborhood. Writes Bolding, "The house is peach and white with boards on the window and a black fence. . . . I'm thinking about the time when the black couple used to stay there and got put out. Now a couple — both doctors — bought the house and had it fixed. There's a rumor that they are taking the workers to court because they don't like the finished work. . . . The only time we see the couple is when they come and pick up the mail."[29]

The effects of gentrification are not restricted to displacement. The process also involves the neighborhood character changing from one familiar to long-term residents to one that matches the aesthetics — in the case of Tremé, French Quarter aesthetics — of the newcomers. Although these changes vary from neighborhood to neighborhood, they often involve a regulation of social spaces, public and private, informal and designated. Examples include newcomers who protest residents' practices of placing house furniture on front porches and congregating outside.

In Tremé, the newcomers' push to make the neighborhood safe, orderly, and well kept becomes most problematic not when monitoring building codes or architectural guidelines but when those efforts collide with the area's musical and parading traditions. One of the earliest and most noted disputes along these lines arose in 1993, when the Association of Residents of Tremé charged that some of the local bars were violating zoning laws. Bar supporters noted the importance of neighborhood taverns in the development of young musicians and the historic association of live music with New Orleans.[30] Such conflicts among music and parading interests, gentrifying residents, and the city have subsequently continued.

The extent to which the influx of new residents, particularly whites, displaces black residents will continue to be debated. Increasing changes in neighborhood character, alienation, and loss of identity associated with gentrification are less debatable. One study suggests that if the gentrification process involved like minorities, this alienation would not occur. The authors support an urban regeneration policy that targets middle-income minority populations, resulting in an effort to "address the race-based concerns of local residents and diffuse racial tensions that might arise due to race politics."[31] While that idea has been promoted in New Orleans, the city's experience proves that racial identity issues are not the same across class.

WHO STOLE THE SOUL?

Father LeDoux was correct in recognizing that the face of gentrification in Tremé was predominantly white. Census data confirm that in Tremé's cultural core (census tract 39), the white population is greater than in census tracts beyond Claiborne. Whites' activities generate very little open hostility from black activists who would like to stem the tide of gentrification. It is as if blacks concede white gentrifying practices because they are consistent with what whites have been doing for decades: buying properties, renovating them, and selling or renting them out at prices the longtime residents cannot afford. Activists are infuriated, however, by the black newcomers, particularly those renovators who have adopted the middle-class suburban aesthetic and appear to have no concern for long-standing residents or the neighborhood's cultural traditions. Activists often include in this group black developers and government officials. Those blacks are cast as worse than gentrifiers: they become race traitors.

The role of blacks as gentrifiers is arguably the most understudied aspect of the phenomenon. Blacks typically are portrayed as the displaced or inconvenienced and not as the agents of housing change. But evidence suggests that blacks were a considerable force in early gentrification movements. By the 1980s, increased housing options for black home buyers led fewer blacks to buy homes in the inner city.[32] The 1990s saw blacks return as gentrifiers, spurred by favorable lending conditions. Tremé was one of the neighborhoods where blacks were buying.

In 2001, the *New Orleans Tribune*, one of the city's African American newspapers, published two issues urging blacks to take part in renovating impoverished neighborhoods. The *Tribune*'s publisher, Beverly McKenna, organized the issues in response to Councilwoman Peggy Wilson's desire to increase the city's tax base by recruiting taxpayers following decades of flight by both blacks and whites. McKenna's plea was expressly race-based: if middle-class blacks failed to do their part to reclaim Tremé, the Seventh Ward, Central City, and other neighborhoods, she argued, they would forever lose their voice and vote. McKenna also argued that the new owners need not live in these areas but could become landlords who would provide "affordable, decent housing for our people."[33]

The PRC agreed with the *Tribune's* idea that African Americans should become involved in historic preservation. Like similar groups in other cities, the PRC was often labeled as an elitist and sometimes racist organization that cared more about buildings than about people. The logical counter to that criticism was to diversify its message and its adherents. The PRC took a different approach to courting African Americans than did the *Tribune*. Instead of appealing to blacks based on a sense of fleeting influence and investment opportunities, the PRC advocated black participation as part of a belief that preservation is good for the community as a whole, particularly economically.

This is not to say that the PRC does not make racially based appeals. In the late 1990s, the center created an African American Historical Preservation Division that has subsequently worked to save the homes of noted jazz musicians and places relevant to the civil rights movement. The PRC's Operation Comeback program and blighted properties workshop are not explicitly race oriented but are more directly concerned with making nontraditional renovators aware of the available financial options.[34]

By the time of the *Tribune's* call, black renovators had become a noticeable force in Tremé as residents and landlords. Most, however, were successful professionals. The *Tribune* and the PRC were trying to extend the process to the middle and lower classes. At the time, the Bynums had already renovated several properties in Tremé and more Uptown. The couple seemed to buy and renovate every available property and to encourage others to do the same. "We try to create a domino effect wherever we invest," explained Naydja Bynum. "We can't control every building in the neighborhood, but we can create an environment that encourages other people to take better care of their property."[35] The Bynums advised people wishing to become successful renovators to purchase homes on the margins of stable areas also undergoing transition.[36] The couple firmly believed that the process provided both aesthetic and economic benefits for the neighborhood and the city. For example, according to Adolph Bynum, the Creole-style house he built generates $2,350 annually in much-needed tax revenue for the city, far more than the $350 generated by the building that formerly occupied the site.[37] The Bynums advised residents concerned about displacement to take advantage of one of the many available programs to bid on houses. The presence of black gentrifiers did not necessarily translate into a reduction of the racial controversy. Black newcomers may have been the same race as longtime residents, but their interests were in many ways largely middle class. They adopted the preservationist ethos and concerned themselves with property values and quality-of-life issues more in line with the concerns of middle-class white residents.

NIGGERS FOR SALE — CHEAP

Advocates for Tremé's longtime black residents voiced their opposition to gentrification as soon as it became evident. They directed their energies not at the white residents but at blacks — particularly Mayor Barthelemy, who was seen as the primary facilitator of Tremé's gentrification — and at those they viewed as complicit in the process. No one was held in higher contempt than Adolph Bynum. Activists took the opportunity to express their displeasure with Bynum at a series of public meetings held by the Preservation of Jazz Advisory Committee in the early 1990s. The meetings were scheduled to keep the public abreast of the developments in the plans for NOJNHP and to give the public an opportunity to comment on the process. Bynum sat on the committee as Tremé's representative. At the first meeting, Hayes explained why he and others were so passionate about what transpired in Armstrong Park. Subsequently, in June 1992, Mitchell drew a line in the sand between activists and longtime residents on the one hand and gentrifiers on the other.[38]

Mitchell often made sweeping statements characterizing jazz and other New Orleans performance traditions as products of Tremé and African Americans (and Africa). Under close scrutiny, Mitchell's claims rest on shaky ground. Many observers summarily dismiss Mitchell because his arguments seem outlandish and his tone impertinent. Even many longtime neighborhood residents consider Mitchell persona non grata, and many others refuse to comment on him, either formally or informally. Mitchell is impossible to ignore, however. Not only is he smart, but he has proven himself wise to the workings of the New Orleans urban political economy. At the June meeting, Mitchell accurately laid out the issues faced by poor and working-class blacks in Tremé, including being priced out of their neighborhoods and facing de facto discrimination:

> Jazz doesn't need to be preserved, it needs to be nurtured. Because and as long as the people of Tremé are allowed to live there with their mothers and their fathers — their grandmothers and their grandfathers and their great-grandmothers and great-grandfathers walk the face of the earth, jazz will continue to happen.

We got misrepresentation on this commission. We got people that have more of an interest in shotgun houses and doubles, in painting houses, and [who] put nothing into what really needs to be done there, not a thing. We are just prettying up buildings. But in prettying up buildings we are bringing people into our community that have no sensitivity to the things that were going on just before they got there. Mr. Bynum, you don't represent Tremé. You don't represent Tremé. You don't represent the people of Tremé. You don't represent the musicians of Tremé. You don't represent their interests. But what you do represent, you represent the interests of people who practice rental discrimination, okay, against your people, okay, like you do. You give us high rents and you say, "Hey, look, we don't want you to be a part of this thing."

We like living good too. We like living in safe, decent, and sanitary housing. You got that, but I can't rent from you. Okay. The people you have associated yourself with . . . put "no children" signs on their buildings. What does that say to me about the people you associate yourself with? That they don't like black people. So what does it tell me about you that you still practice the color [caste] system, that you still think that we are living in post-Reconstruction? You don't support us. You know nothing about the people of Tremé. . . .

You throw a brick and hide. You don't stand up for the little people. You talk about jazz. Well, that old man has been in that community, Mr. Bynum, since 1946 as a businessman and a property owner. Okay, and the hypocrisy — the politics of this makes a hypocrisy for some of the decent work done by some of the people on the commission. Your presence is hypocrisy.[39]

Activists also took exception to the local government's efforts to stimulate housing development in Tremé. During the Barthelemy administration, activists targeted the ARC. In the spring of 1993, the Brotherhood of the TU circulated a profanity-filled flyer headed "NIGGERS FOR SALE CHEAP — IN TREMÉ" that denounced and threatened the people involved in the ARC. The flyer singled out Juakali, ARC board member Joan Rhodes, and Adolph Bynum for their roles in plotting to sell Tremé "out from underneath" the black community. Specifically, it called for Juakali to be run out of the neighborhood and for people to boycott Rhodes's funeral businesses.

WE URGE YOU TO BOYCOTT ALL RHODES BUSINESSES! THIS NIGGER FOR SALE — CHEAP, IS USING THE MONEY FROM POOR BLACKS' INSURANCE, FUNERALS, AND LIMOUSINE RENTALS TO HURT THESE SAME PEOPLE. SHE WANTS ALL POOR BLACK RENTERS OUT OF THE TREMÉ AND SHE IS SELLING BLACK PEOPLE

OUT TO IT. . . . WE MEAN BUSINESS. ALL YOU SELL OUT NIGGERS MEETING WITH
THAT HO SIDNEY AND HAVING SECRET MEETINGS TO SELL OUT TREMÉ BETTER
KNOW THIS — TREMÉ IS THE BIGGEST BLACK FAMILY IN THE CITY OF NEW
ORLEANS. . . . THIS IS YOUR FIRST AND LAST WARNING! POOR BLACK RENTERS
IN TREMÉ ARE NOT GOING ANYWHERE! AND IF ANYTHING OR ANYBODY TRIES
TO MOVE THEM, WE PROMISE TO TAKE TREMÉ WITH THEM — STARTING WITH
ALL YOU SELL OUT NIGGERS FOR SALE CHEAP!!!!!!!!!![40]

Tremé residents have subsequently continued to voice concerns regarding increasing gentrification and its effect on poor black residents that match the sentiments of the flyer.

In the eyes of most activists, Morial's housing policy, as administered by Sylvain, was no better than Barthelemy's. Even though the Impact Neighborhood Strategy made provisions for low-income homeowners to improve their properties, the administration was largely seen as an advocate for gentrification. The Villa and its fence were perceived as serving those efforts. Furthermore, the federal government money that funded the Villa was viewed as misused for patronage jobs instead of affordable housing. Not only activists but long-time residents felt this way. Even though the museum saw itself as open to the neighborhood and made outreach efforts, many community members simply felt unwelcome there.

With this knowledge of Tremé's housing landscape and history, I ventured into the Ninth Ward on that Sunday afternoon in 2003. I was curious to see if the honorary king of the Nine Times parade was Tremé's Adolph Bynum. It was. After a little music from the Hot 8 Brass Band, he stepped from the bar door in full costume. With champagne glass in hand, Bynum did his best second line to a waiting car. For the next few hours, the parade wound through the streets of the Ninth Ward, and I wondered whether the area's residents knew about the controversy that surrounded Bynum in Tremé.

In the last years of his term, Marc Morial, like his father, tried unsuccessfully to find a way around the city's two-term limit. In 2002, New Orleans elected local cable television executive Ray Nagin as its new mayor. Nagin is New Orleans's fourth African American mayor but the first without deep Seventh Ward roots. He is also not a career politician. Nagin entered office as a business-friendly mayor in the mold of Barthelemy. In fact, Nagin won the election with 80 percent of the white vote and 40 percent of the black vote. Part of his mission was to weed out the perceived corruption and blatant, excessive patronage of the Morial administration. During Nagin's first few years in office, the New Orleans African American Museum was shut down because of suspicion of misused funds, effectively ending the Morial administration's involvement in Tremé. In 2003, Nagin began holding neighborhood meetings to gauge resident concerns. Tremé's residents voiced familiar concerns, including gentrification, which showed no signs of slowing. During the first part of his term, Nagin did not develop a strong Tremé housing initiative, and the destruction caused by Hurricane Katrina in 2005 set off a series of events that threaten to accelerate the residential changes already under way there.

Epilogue

Post-Katrina Tremé

As I do every year, I spent much of the summer of 2005 in New Orleans. Summer in the city is not necessarily pleasant, since the heat and humidity stifle much of what is good about being there. My visit, however, was quite productive, as I collected information and conducted interviews to round out the story of Tremé. I also attended a city council meeting convened explicitly to discuss the controversy surrounding the New Orleans Police Department's disruption of an annual Mardi Gras Indian tradition that occurs every spring on the evening of St. Joseph's Day. On that night, for reasons not fully understood, Mardi Gras Indians take to the streets, guided only by streetlamps and flashlights. Before Super Bowl Sunday parades and before Indians donned their suits year-round for musical performances and events such as Jazz Fest, St. Joseph's Day was the second and final time Indians wore their suits before they were disassembled each year.

In 2005, however, police used sirens, flashing lights, and by some accounts cars to clear the St. Joseph's Day Indians and their followers from the streets. Witnesses also accused the police of being verbally abusive in ordering people off the street and in demanding that Indians remove their suits. Participants and observers perceived the police as dangerously and disrespectfully disrupting a long-standing cultural practice. For their part, the police claimed to be responding to a report of an Indian carrying a gun and cited the Indians' lack of a permit in ordering them off the streets. Months later, the incident remained fresh in the minds of Indians who met regularly to discuss the situation.[1]

On 27 June, the city council convened a public meeting to clear the air regarding the situation. The meeting itself was not explicitly related to Tremé: the incident in question happened Uptown. But the larger issue — the manner in which the local government regarded the city's African American performance traditions — was directly related to Tremé, where such traditions have a long history. The meeting was tense from the start, as Tremé activist Jerome Smith barked in protest when a group of black children was momentarily prevented from making a presentation to the council. Smith's insistence that the children should be treated "as if they were President [George W.] Bush's children" reveals the extent to which the relationship between City Hall and the African American community was about respect as much as anything else.[2]

Following the opening remarks, the first person to address the council was Allison "Tootie" Montana, big chief of the Yellow Pocahontas Mardi Gras Indian tribe. Montana, known as the chief of chiefs, was arguably the most noted figure in the Mardi Gras Indian tradition. Standing before the council, Montana called for a new, more civil tone in the relationship between the city and the various cultural performance traditions. Before he could finish, Montana collapsed and slumped to the ground. As paramedics attended to the fallen man, Big Chief Larry Bannock of the Golden Star Hunters led the members of countless Indian tribes, second-line clubs, and the various other traditional cultural groups in attendance in singing the Mardi Gras Indian prayer, "Indian Red." Montana gave his last breath advocating on behalf of New Orleans's African American performance traditions.[3]

Montana's funeral was a special event. Indian funerals are fairly rare, reserved primarily for the big chiefs of Mardi Gras Indian tribes. They contain elements of traditional jazz funerals but differ in important ways. For example, Indian funerals do not necessarily include brass bands, whereas a jazz funeral must by definition have music.

Following a service at Tremé's St. Augustine Roman Catholic Church, the funeral procession passed by Montana's house before heading down Claiborne Avenue to St. Louis Cemetery No. II. There, in the narrow pathways between vaults and tombs, Father Jerome LeDoux said his final words over Montana's casket as people looked down from atop other tombs. Montana's funeral was the only Downtown funeral I ever attended that ended in one of the St. Louis cemeteries; all of the other burials have taken place in suburban cemeteries to which it is too far to walk, necessarily truncating the traditional funeral parade experience. The events that led to Montana's death and those that followed demonstrate that the city's African American performance traditions were alive and well, as was the city of New Orleans's ambivalent and contradictory stance toward those traditions. Not a month later, however, the issue of police harassment at second-line parades would seem trivial when the future of the city itself was at stake. Hurricane Katrina has had very definite implications for New Orleans's culture and traditions, including the uncertain futures of its practitioners and the survival of those traditions in the places they have historically been practiced.

Unlike New Orleans's lower-lying neighborhoods, Tremé escaped complete inundation by the floodwaters. The neighborhood's location in relation to the high ground of the Mississippi River's natural levee and the Esplanade Ridge mitigated the damage seen in parts of the neighborhood closer to the French Quarter. As a result, some neighborhood landmarks, including the Back Street Museum and St. Augustine, escaped with no flood damage, although the church was damaged by high winds. Waterlines grew higher approaching Claiborne Avenue and on toward Broad. Noted Claiborne Avenue area businesses, including the Charbonnet Funeral Home, Ernie K-Doe's Mother-in-Law Lounge, and most notably the Circle Food Store, took on several feet of water. Beyond Claiborne Avenue, the damage from standing water was more severe. In the months following the storm, Claiborne Avenue represented something of a dividing line. The area stretching from the river to Claiborne — the unflooded high ground — comprised what became known as the sliver on the river. In that area, residents soon returned and businesses resumed surprisingly quickly, though initially without such amenities as ice, proper silverware, and credit card service. The area from Claiborne to the lake, conversely, remained largely dark and sparsely inhabited.

Katrina affected New Orleans's residents in a variety of ways, causing residential dislocation, psychological distress, and financial ruin, all complicated by the complete collapse of the city's vital services and infrastructure. The level of devastation and the inevitability of future hurricanes has led people to ask serious questions about the city's future. On 10 September 2005, I took part in a conversation on the op-ed page of the *New York Times*. The other essays, written by geographer Craig Colten, engineering professor Henry Petroski, and former secretary of the interior Bruce Babbitt, advocated environmental and engineering solutions to keep New Orleans dry and safe.[4] I wrote about the right of New Orleans's working-class African Americans to return to the city.[5]

Mayor Ray Nagin officially opened New Orleans for return on 30 September. At the time, tens of thousands of the city's residents remained scattered across the country, unsure of whether they could or would return. In New Orleans, people began planning their futures, including addressing the question of whether to relocate or rebuild their homes. Businesses, organizations, and institutions faced the same issues. Nagin created the Bring New Orleans Back Commission to lay out a plan to guide the city's reconstruction. In addition to targeting basic infrastructure and services, the commission sought to repair New Orleans's cultural economy through the efforts of a sixteen-member Culture Committee cochaired by attorney Cesar Burgos and jazz musician Wynton Marsalis. The committee set out to achieve five objectives:

1. rebuild our talent pool of artists, cultural groups, and cultural entrepreneurs;

2. support community-based cultural traditions and repair and develop cultural facilities;

3. market New Orleans as a world-class cultural capital;

4. teach our arts and cultural traditions to our young people;

5. attract new investment from national and international sources.[6]

Not surprisingly, members of the New Orleans cultural community did not wait for the committee's report. Writers, photographers, chefs, and others resumed their practices as soon as they returned to the city or wherever else they found themselves. African American parading traditions also returned to the streets in October with a memorial parade for noted chef Austin Leslie, who had died while away from the city. That same month, the Prince of Wales Social Aid and Pleasure Club held its anniversary parade. These early parades were out of sorts, varying from their usual starting locations, routes, and racial demographics as a consequence of Katrina's impact on the population and landscape.[7] The health of the city's unique cultural practices, especially those tied to the displaced African American population, remained a concern as the year came to a close.

On a weekday evening in January 2006, I sat on stage at Loyola University–New Orleans with some of the city's most noted scholars and cultural icons, including chef Susan Spicer, professors John Biguenet and Alecia Long, author and *Times-Picayune* columnist Lolis Eric Elie, and Louisiana blues legend Eddie Bo. The occasion was the first in a series of panel discussions about the state of New Orleans following Hurricane Katrina. The panel addressed the question, "New Orleans Culture: Can It Be Saved?" Generously billed as an expert on New Orleans's African American parading organizations, I was expected, in my estimation, to contribute to a discussion about the future of second-line parading. Elie and Long dominated the evening with eloquent statements about the uniqueness and resilience of New Orleans culture. The solidly Uptown audience affirmed these positions with repeated rounds of applause. As I expected, I was asked about the future of neighborhood-based parading. I told those assembled that I saw the threat to parading as being inseparable from the return of New Orleans's African American population. I added that I believed that gentrification had threatened New Orleans culture, or at least that portion of it actively and organically produced in African American neighborhoods, since long before the storm. I also pointed that in neighborhoods with historic architecture, the danger to the tradition would be even greater if houses passed from rental stock to owner occupancy. Other panelists presented a more optimistic scenario, and the evening failed to produce a basic, sustained conversation about New Orleans culture.

Despite its shortcomings, the evening closed with the understanding that everything was not well with the performance traditions of New Orleans's working-class African Americans. One of the final questions from the audience came from a member of the Prince of Wales Social Aid and Pleasure Club who explained that in the wake of Katrina, the police department had raised the permit fees paid by parading organizations from sixteen hundred dollars to forty-four hundred dollars. Such a policy, enacted when many of the affected or interested parties were not even in the city, has the potential to take African American performance traditions off the street.

The root cause of the fee increase was a violent incident at the conclusion of an All Star Second Line on 15 January 2006. The parade had been a symbolic reclaiming of the streets by more than thirty different social aid and pleasure clubs. Organizers also sought to make a statement regarding the right of the displaced to return to New Orleans and to obtain city services. Estimates placed parade attendance as high as eight thousand, many of them Katrina evacuees who returned from near and far to attend the parade. Unfortunately, unrelated gunshots marred the parade's conclusion. The New Orleans Police Department announced the fee increase almost immediately, justifying the action as necessary to cover the cost of paying for police escorts at a time when the city was short of both money and officers. The parading organizations, however, felt that the increase was a burden to the working-class organizations and that it threatened to eliminate second-line parading as a viable mode of expression. With the assistance of the American Civil Liberties Union, the Social Aid and Pleasure Club Task Force sued the City of New Orleans for violating paraders' First Amendment rights.[8] The lawsuit was settled out of court in April 2007, with the task force winning the right to hold the city accountable for the fees incurred for parading permits. While the decision to raise parade permit fees may not have been designed directly to affect Tremé, it is difficult not to view the Archdiocese of New Orleans's decision to close St. Augustine Parish in this light.

On 6 February 2006, the archdiocese announced its intention immediately to close the doors of seven parishes, including St. Augustine, as part of a larger "pastoral plan." The decision was part of an ongoing review process, Catholic Life 2000, as well as of a post-Katrina review requested by Archbishop Alfred

Hughes to provide the archdiocese with information about parish buildings and data on returning parishioners. The information-gathering mission began at an October 2005 meeting between the archbishop and the archdiocese's twelve deaneries. The ultimate goal was to develop a plan to reopen churches over the next few years, and the plan did not specifically call for the closing of St. Augustine. In fact, the church would remain open as a worship space, but the formal parish would close. Territorially, St. Augustine would become part of St. Peter Claver Parish, also in Tremé.[9]

Not long after the announcement, St. Augustine parishioners, led by Sandra Gordon, president of the parish's Pastoral Council, offered an impressive and well-organized response. In March 2006, the council fired off several letters to Archbishop Hughes protesting the pending closing. Most compellingly, the group questioned whether the parish-closing process could be "reconciled with [the justifications] prescribed by Canon Law."[10] According to Canon Law, when a parish or "community of the faithful" is established, it becomes "a public juridic person" and is entitled to permanence unless the diocesan bishop has "just cause" for its modification. To determine whether the process was arbitrary, the Pastoral Council requested "any and all documentation, including but not limited to, agendas[,] minutes[,] parties present, notes, reports, transcriptions, audiotapes, videotapes or any other records pertaining to the change in status of St. Augustine Parish."[11]

On 20 March, twelve activists began a siege of the parish rectory. One week later, Father Michael Jacques, accompanied by the Reverend William Maestri, entered St. Augustine to deliver morning mass. Confronted by a boisterous and angry congregation, Maestri ordered the mass halted. It was later revealed that Maestri and Jacques had been accompanied to St. Augustine by nearly two dozen armed and unarmed undercover policemen, further incensing community members.[12]

Following mediated negotiations, St. Augustine reopened on 8 April. As part of the negotiations, Father Ledoux relocated to Our Mother of Mercy church in Ft. Worth, Texas, and was replaced by the Reverend Quentin Moody. The church also received a set of benchmarks that it would have to meet to be considered viable and remain open. In the spring of 2009, St. Augustine received word from the archdiocese that it had been removed from probation.[13]

LAFITTE

The increased parading fees and the attempt to close St. Augustine illustrate the changes that affected New Orleans residents in the wake of Hurricane Katrina.

Furthermore, both situations highlight the ways in which working-class African Americans, who were affected disproportionately by the storm, are continually and consistently on the receiving end of decisions that affect their daily lives without the benefit of their input. Other changes, particularly in the landscape, have an even greater potential to affect the long-term residents of Tremé. These changes include the demolition of the Lafitte public housing development to the rear of Tremé's cultural core and the ongoing efforts to redevelop Rampart Street.

As of this writing, a long stretch of Orleans Avenue lies vacant. For more than seventy years, the site had been occupied by the Lafitte public housing development, one of ten such developments constructed in New Orleans as a consequence of New Deal housing legislation that would build publicly owned housing across the United States. The program, designed to provide American citizens with decent and affordable places to live, has been deeply troubled since the 1960s. Instead of serving as a way station for the working class, as originally intended, public housing became an intergenerational refuge for the chronically poor. As more and more whites left public housing, much of which had been segregated, the program became increasingly stigmatized as a failed government handout for pathologically impoverished African Americans. Drug epidemics, violent crime, and illegitimacy were but a few of the issues that made life in public housing undesirable, even intolerable. For their part, federal and local governments allowed the housing to deteriorate to unlivable conditions. Furthermore, in countless cities, including New Orleans, public housing was plagued by local corruption and ineptitude. It is not surprising, then, that for years before Katrina, the Housing Authority of New Orleans (HANO) had been under federal control.

There are, nevertheless, compelling stories of public housing developments as successful neighborhoods and communities. For every drug deal, murder, or unwed mother that makes news, there are countless untold stories of productive citizens — heroes, community leaders, and everyday folk — creating social networks that allow people to survive without the resources that middle-class Americans take for granted. Lafitte was no different.

The nation's public housing program received a boost with the creation of the HOPE VI program in 1992. HOPE VI promised to revolutionize public housing by revitalizing deteriorating, institutionalized housing developments. In most cases, revitalization involves demolition of existing housing and reconstitution of the development on the same site as a mixed-income community of owners and tenants. Furthermore, HOPE VI projects also included private business components.[14]

Prior to Hurricane Katrina, New Orleans's Fischer and St. Thomas developments underwent the HOPE VI renovation process, the latter with a great deal of controversy over the project's inclusion of a Super Wal-Mart. Before the hurricane struck, three additional New Orleans developments (St. Bernard, B. W. Cooper [Magnolia], and C. J. Peete [Magnolia]) were slated for demolition. Following Hurricane Katrina, HANO added Lafitte to the list.

To an even greater extent than the St. Augustine controversy, the scheduled demolition of the Lafitte and New Orleans's other remaining public housing developments garnered national attention. Progressive voices in the city, in the national media, and on the Internet viewed the pending closures and demolition as another injustice inflicted on the city's poor African Americans. Specific objections to the plan included the development's eligibility for listing on the National Register of Historic Places (and provisions required by the Historic Preservation Act for structures identified as such); the violation of residents' civil and property rights by HANO and by the U.S. Department of Housing and Urban Development (HUD); and the danger to the historic cultural fabric of the Tremé neighborhood.

Housing activists' most compelling objection, and possibly the reason for the national attention, concerned the city's housing shortage. Although the extent of storm damage differed for each development, many observers believed that repairing these developments and making use of undamaged units provided the quickest and cheapest way to address the city's housing shortage, which was so dire that workers helping to rebuild the city lived on cruise ships docked on the Mississippi River.

The decision to add the Lafitte to the list of public housing developments scheduled for demolition fit nicely in the prevailing post-Katrina redevelopment philosophy, which viewed the disaster as a chance for New Orleans to wipe the slate clean and fix its ills. With many of the city's perceived "problem residents" relocated across the country and with the inevitable influx of federal redevelopment dollars, New Orleans, like the phoenix, could rise from the ashes. Many people expressed such views, including those who saw Katrina as God's retribution for the city's sinful ways; members of Congress, who would ultimately have to pay for the rebuilding of the city; and local residents tired of New Orleans's high crime rate. Proponents of these views advocated policies such as letting the city sink, not rebuilding the Ninth Ward, and not rebuilding public housing. Many of these views resonated with poorly concealed racist sentiments about New Orleans's African American population.

Some of the voices against public housing — or at least against public housing as it had existed prior to the storm — came from African American city council members. At a 20 February 2006 meeting of the council's Housing Committee, three members spoke in support of HUD's new screening process that required potential returning residents to make a commitment to work. At the meeting, HANO chief Nadine Jarmon said, "Part of the process is asking about people's ability or willingness to work. If someone says, 'well my income qualifies me for public housing and I want to come home' but they don't express a willingness to work, or they weren't working before Katrina, then you're making a decision to pass over those people." Added Councilman Oliver Thomas, "We don't need soap opera watchers right now. We're going to target the people who are going to work. Its not that I'm fed up, but that at some point there has to be a whole new level of motivation, and people have got to stop blaming the government for something they ought to do."[15]

These sentiments are easy to critique as playing into decades-old stereotypes about public housing residents that ignore many of the harsh realities of life in public housing and the inner city. Furthermore, these comments appear opportunistic in the face of disaster. Both parties were essentially contending that nonworking public housing residents were problematic and that those residents should become some other city's problem.

For the next two years, HUD/HANO and New Orleans housing activists argued their positions in the court of public opinion. Demolition/redevelopment advocates pushed for a better quality of life, while opponents stuck with the themes of dispossession, housing shortage, and racial injustice. Loyola lawyer Bill Quigley presented the progressive housing position effectively in print and through the electronic media.[16] On the ground, activists (many of whom migrated to the city following Katrina) stood shoulder to shoulder with disgruntled public housing residents. In late November 2007, however, HANO entered into $31 million worth of contracts with several construction companies for the demolition of the majority of New Orleans's public housing stock. The following month, Democratic U.S. Senators Harry Reid and Barack Obama and Congresswoman Nancy Pelosi petitioned President Bush to delay demolition of New Orleans public housing. In the end, all attempts to halt demolition failed, and Lafitte was razed. Once again, entire blocks of Tremé have been flattened. It is uncertain what will happen to the development's former residents or what the new Lafitte will look like.

As chapter 7 argues, the presence of the Iberville and Lafitte public housing developments and to a lesser extent the elevated Interstate 10 helped to prevent Tremé's gentrification. With the demise of one of those "disincentives to gentrification" and with its replacement unlikely to represent the same danger to real estate investors and speculators, Tremé and the Sixth Ward may seem more appealing, especially when coupled with the ongoing changes across the neighborhood on Rampart Street.

RAMPART STREET

Rampart functions as a liminal space, sharing qualities of both the French Quarter and Tremé. According to Kathleen O'Reilly and Michael Crutcher, "It is on Rampart Street that well-policed, heterosexual tourist space, marginal gay entertainment spaces, and spaces marked Black mingle together."[17] Historically, however, Rampart Street began to assume an "undesirable" character in the early twentieth century, contemporaneous with the veneration of the Vieux Carré and the subsequent denigration of Tremé. From that point onward, Rampart was conceived as being more like Tremé. As the French Quarter has become more gentrified and with issues of preservation being taken more seriously throughout the larger Quarter, the desire for Rampart Street to have its own renaissance has become more pressing.

Concern about crime on Rampart reached its zenith in the late 1990s, when several high-profile murders took place there. In October 1997, a man died after being shot two weeks earlier at the corner of Rampart and Barracks. Less than a year later, another man was shot on Governor Nicholls, in the vicinity of Rampart. Both men were locals, gunned down while engaged in the mundane chores of walking a dog and grocery shopping, respectively. The second murder prompted a letter to the editor of the *New Orleans Times-Picayune* asking for more policing on Rampart. The author of this letter recognized Rampart as a permeable boundary frequently crossed or transgressed by young criminals, claiming to have "witnessed and pursued numerous juveniles who entered the quarter by way of Rampart St., committed criminal acts, and then fled to safety across Rampart."[18]

This view of Rampart as a gateway into the French Quarter for criminals from outside neighborhoods is not a new idea. It is the same understanding of Rampart that informs the experience of traveling from the French Quarter across the threshold of Rampart and into Faubourg Tremé. Crime, however, is only one of the issues surrounding Rampart Street. More important in the long run is what kind of street Rampart will become if it is revitalized — that is, whether it will be oriented toward art and culture or toward live music. Considering New Orleans's musical heritage and the importance of music to the local culture and tourist economy, creating an environment where live music can thrive would appear to be of paramount importance. As with parading, however, the city seems to be trying to make it difficult for live music to flourish.

By the late 1990s, North Rampart could be considered a peripheral tourist destination within the French Quarter where authentic local music could be found. Donna's Bar and Grill at St. Ann and Rampart dubbed itself the city's brass band headquarters, while the next block featured a new jazz club, the Funky Butt at Congo Square. The two establishments provided a basis for the North Rampart Street entertainment district. French Quarter residents, however, had designs for Rampart that did not include live music.

In October 2002, neighborhood residents expressed their dissatisfaction with the New Orleans Planning Commission's inclusion of the Quarter side of North Rampart as an "an entertainment district lined with bars and live music clubs." Objections forced the commission to edit a map of the proposed area to show "arts and culture" rather than entertainment as the street's projected use.[19] At the time, development on North Rampart Street was poised to take off. A September 2004 *Times-Picayune* article reported the area's rebirth, driven by cheap residential real estate prices. In addition, several larger projects had been announced and approved, most notably a multiunit residential development at the corner of Rampart and Esplanade.[20] The effort to limit live music can be seen as French Quarter residents' attempt to shape the character of the revitalization.

French Quarter residents were not the only people concerned about live music on North Rampart. City Hall became involved when police began cracking down on the street's music clubs after a neighborhood meeting at which residents sought a solution to the recent proliferation of live music venues and (gay) bars. Residents decided that closer policing of zoning regulations was the best method for reducing unwanted music on Rampart. In particular, residents sought to close bars that lacked live music permits. The tightened enforcement highlighted an ongoing controversy about music's role in the local economy that pitted resident groups and city leaders against each other. Rampart Street property owner Leo Watermeier argued, "Nobody wants another Bourbon Street there, but from all we can tell, we feel that hasn't detracted at all from life in this part of the Quarter." The president of the Vieux Carré Property Owners, Residents, and Associates, Nathan Chapman, countered, "It is not these clubs that have brought back North Rampart Street; it's been normal economic expansion. The main thing now, at every meeting I go to, people talk about enforcement of the law, and that area is not zoned for live entertainment." City council member Jackie Clarkson asserted that tighter enforcement was "not designed to pick on music places or on North Rampart Street. This is a problem throughout the French Quarter and the entire city. It's illegal T-shirts, and illegal alcohol and illegal bed-and-breakfasts, and illegal music. I'm picking on all the above and we're going to get tough."[21]

Hurricane Katrina halted the North Rampart renaissance, and the controversy surrounding live music permits ebbed for a time. North Rampart itself did not flood, but the disruption caused by the storm upset its real estate market and entertainment scene. In addition, the city was burdened with issues larger than checking entertainment permits. Almost two years after the hurricane, community interest in the North Rampart area resurfaced. The nonprofit North Rampart Main Street Association, which grew out of the Organization for Renaissance on Rampart, partnered with the annual Satchmo SummerFest to sponsor an event highlighting efforts to improve North Rampart Street and introducing the Friends of North Rampart program, which was charged with making actual improvements to the street. In 2007 and again in 2008, the group sponsored the North Rampart Street Festival, complete with vendors, artists, and live music. The festival sought to create a sense of pride and awareness about North Rampart Street and to showcase the improvements to Armstrong Park after Katrina.

Critics have questioned the association's motivations, mainly because the group has championed the position on live music espoused by Clarkson and various French Quarter groups. According to North Rampart Main Street Association copresident Sue Klein, if more bars are allowed on North Rampart, the street "might end up as low-end nighttime economy. I think we can see what happened on Bourbon Street."[22] One of the most effective voices in support of the arts is Jan Ramsey, publisher and editor in chief of New Orleans's main music and culture magazine, *Offbeat*. In a June 2007 editorial, Ramsey assessed what she believes are North Rampart's problems: "It's heartbreaking to know that we have a city that gives lip service [to] its music — and uses it to attract visitors — [but] doesn't really do anything to make this a 'real' music city. One easy change would be to make sure that there's zoning on North Rampart that allows live music performance." She continues, "The French Quarter citizens who don't want anything to change on North Rampart are not doing the Vieux Carre or the city of New Orleans any favors. They don't have any love for New Orleans culture, except for their expensive historic French Quarter digs. They just want to live in an area that's quiet. I say, if you don't like the musical 'noise' then go live in the suburbs and let the music play."[23]

Whether the association can turn Rampart around remains to be seen. Over the years, many initiatives have targeted the area, but none has had lasting success. The association's affiliation with the state and national Main Street program increases its likelihood of success. If Rampart is revitalized, it will cease to be a barrier to investment in the same way that Lafitte is no longer a barrier.

I do not argue that large parts of the city should be left in decay just to preserve New Orleans's cultural traditions. However, spatial processes and changes in the landscape affect daily life. The incidents presented in this chapter do a poor job of incorporating the input of poor and minority populations in decisions that affect their lives. Furthermore, the arguments against public housing, parading, and live music uncritically link certain behaviors to certain racial groups and economic classes.

Two legacies have the potential to shape Tremé: one is architectural and material; the other is social and cultural. This contrived separation fails under critical scrutiny but exists in the everyday. To the preservationist and gentrifier, individual historic structures and neighborhoods of such structures are valuable assets on the urban landscape. The renovation of dilapidated structures, an end to the demolition of historic sites, and the development of creative financing for home purchases and renovations are some of the methods preservationists and gentrifiers use to create the environments they seek. Longer-term residents and community activists, by contrast, see themselves and their culture as the precious resource, believing that preservation must include efforts to improve residents' quality of life, create economic opportunities, and protect and foster local cultural traditions.

The corner of Ursuline and Robertson in Tremé is now quiet. Several years have passed since Joe's Cozy Corner closed. The building still stands, minus the awning, shoe-shine stand, and posted messages about what behaviors are not permitted on the premises. The present owner has restored the structure to some historic ideal, including removal of a brick facade that was not original. Left untouched is a remnant of an old advertisement painted on the side of the structure, typical of early-twentieth-century painted ads on commercial buildings. A few blocks away, the Little People's Place is mostly shuttered as well, open only on certain dates, such as Mardi Gras. Presently, the only notable regularly scheduled music performance in the interior or residential part of Tremé is the Tremé Brass Band's weekly performance at the Candlelight Lounge.

Maybe it is a coincidence that the decline of entertainment venues in the interior or revisionist residential sections of Tremé is being countered by a rebirth of sorts on St. Bernard Avenue. If the past decade or so is any indication, architecture will trump culture. But the people of Tremé are likely to continue fighting to maintain their presence in the landscape.

NOTES

PREFACE

1. Mitchell, "End of Public Space?"; Ruddick, "Constructing Difference"; Staeheli and Thompson, "Community, Citizenship, and Struggles."

2. Habermas, *Structural Transformation*; Fraser, "Rethinking the Public Sphere"; Lefebvre, *Production of Space*; Harvey, *Condition of Postmodernity*; Castells, *City and the Grassroots*.

3. Zukin, *Culture of Cities*; Sorkin, *Variations on a Theme Park*; Knox, *Restless Urban Landscape*.

4. hooks, *Yearning*; hooks and West, *Breaking Bread*; Fraser, "Rethinking the Public Sphere," 67.

5. Blassingame, "Before the Ghetto," 484–85.

6. Blassingame, *Black New Orleans*.

7. Goings and Mohl, *New African American Urban History*, 3.

8. Ibid.; Journal of Urban History 21, nos. 3–4 (1995).

9. Soja, *Postmodern Geographies*, 77.

10. White, "'It Was a Proud Day'"; Earl Lewis, "Connecting Memory"; Brown and Kimball, "Mapping the Terrain."

11. Castells, *City and the Grassroots*, 317.

12. Haymes, *Race, Culture, and City*, 144.

13. Groth and Wilson, "Polyphony."

14. Schein, *Landscape and Race*.

INTRODUCTION

1. *New Orleans Police Department: 2004 Yearly Crime Statistics*, www.cityofno.com/pg-50-12-2004-yearly-crime-statistics.aspx (accessed 23 April 2008).

2. Parades traditionally are sponsored by neighborhood-based groups called social aid and pleasure clubs (or social and pleasure clubs). However, parades, like jazz funerals, do not always have sponsoring clubs.

3. Reckdahl, "Down on the Corner."

4. C. Atkinson, "Whose New Orleans?," 94.

5. For an interesting look at the importance of neighborhood-level places in New Orleans, see Breunlin, Himelstein, and Rogers, Cornerstones.

6. Berquin-Duvallon cited in Sublette, *World That Made New Orleans*, 243.

7. Scherman, *Backbeat*, 70.

8. T. Young, "Man Shot"; City of New Orleans, Mayor's Office of Communications, Alcohol Board Revokes Permit.

9. Parekh, "Inhabiting Tremé."

CHAPTER 1. CREATING BLACK TREMÉ

1. New Orleans's geographic orientation is essential to understanding discussions of the city. *Uptown* generally denotes upriver, while *Downtown* denotes downriver. The other major directions are not east and west but river and lake.

2. O'Reilly and Crutcher, "Parallel Politics."

3. Crutcher, "Protecting 'Place'"; Huaracha, "Evolution of a Public Open Space."

4. Mohl, "Planned Destruction."

5. The ward system was initiated in 1805, which predates most significant expansions of the Quarter. Tremé was not included in the ward system until 1847. The present ward configuration is largely based on changes dating to 1852, when New Orleans's three municipal districts were consolidated. The configuration has changed little since the annexation of Carrolton in 1880.

6. Bureau of Governmental Research, *Wards of New Orleans*, 21.

7. Ibid., 22.

8. Cohn, *Triksta*, 19. Residents of the nearby Melpomene (Guste) housing project also identify with the Third Ward.

9. Nelson, *Combination*; Bolding, *Before and after N. Dorgenois*.

10. http://www.neworleansonline.com/tools/neighborhoodguide/ (accessed 12 October 2008).

11. *Living With History in New Orleans's Neighborhoods: Tremé*, http://www.prcno. org/neighborhoods/brochures/Treme.pdf (accessed 8 October 2008).

12. M. Smith, *Mardi Gras Indians*.

13. Norman Smith, interview, 28 July 1994, Tremé Oral History Collection, Amistad Research Center, Tulane University.

14. For works about Tremé-area Creoles who passed as white, see Broyard, *One Drop* (on literary critic Anatole Broyard); Boxer, "Herriman" (on cartoonist George Herriman).

15. Herczog, *Frommer's New Orleans*, 90; Downs, *Lonely Planet*, 13; Fodor's *New Orleans*, 49.

16. Cangelosi, "Which Way Tremé?"

17. Haymes, *Race, Culture, and City*, 10.

CHAPTER 2. AFRO-CREOLE TREMÉ

1. "Cuban Refugees Arrive Destitute."

2. Lachance, "1809 Immigration."

3. Bell, *Revolution, Romanticism, and the Afro-Creole Protest Tradition*; Hall, *Africans in Colonial Louisiana*; Blassingame, *Black New Orleans*; Hirsch and Logsdon, *Creole New Orleans*; Long, *Great Southern Babylon*; Kein, *Creole*; Hanger, *Bounded Lives, Bounded Places.*

4. Hall, *Africans in Colonial Louisiana*, 41.

5. Ibid., 177.

6. Ingersoll, "View from the Parish Jail."

7. Hall, *Africans in Colonial Louisiana*, 15.

8. Johnson, "New Orleans's Congo Square."

9. Johnson, "Colonial New Orleans."

10. For more on the Natchez massacre, see Hall, *Africans in Colonial Louisiana.*

11. Hirsch and Logsdon, *Creole New Orleans*, 189.

12. Martin, "*Plaçage*," 57–70.

13. In Louisiana, Creole can be a contentious concept, both within the African-descended population and between white and black Creoles. For more on the latter, see Dominguez, *White by Definition.*

14. Bell, *Revolution, Romanticism, and the Afro-Creole Protest Tradition*, 16.

15. Ibid., 33.

16. Hall, *Africans in Colonial Louisiana*, 379.

17. Robin quoted in ibid., 380.

18. Christovich and Toledano, *Faubourg Tremé and Bayou Road*, xi.

19. Ibid., 57.

20. Ibid., 60.

21. Martin, "*Plaçage*," 65.

22. Bryan, "Marcus Christian's Treatment"; Dunbar-Nelson, "People of Color," pts. 1 and 2; Barthelemy, "Light, Bright, Damn Near White"; Anthony, "Lost Boundaries."

23. Dominguez, *White by Definition.*

24. Tregle, "Creoles and Americans," 154; Campanella, *Time and Place*, 117–20.

25. Tregle, "Creoles and Americans." The first municipality included the French Quarter and the Faubourg Tremé. The second district included the Faubourg St. Marie and other areas upriver of Canal Street and served the new American population. The third municipality, downriver from the first, was analogous to Creole Faubourg Marigny. The new municipalities controlled only "internal financial and economic affairs" (156), and all three were overseen by one mayor and a single police force. Downtown Creoles likely saw the creation of New Orleans's municipal system as a victory or at least as a reprieve from the American onslaught. The 1830s, 1840s, and 1850s saw declining influence for the French Quarter and Creole culture in general. Most glaringly, the Creole sector fell behind in commercial wealth. In addition, Creole failures in education translated into Creole absences from certain professions and the declining use of the French language. The creation of a separate Creole enclave could not stop American political, economic, and demographic progress.

26. Logsdon and Bell, "Americanization," 207.

27. Johnson, "New Orleans's Congo Square," 39.

28. Ibid.

29. Latrobe, *Impressions Respecting New Orleans*, 121–28.

30. Johnson, "New Orleans's Congo Square," 140.

31. Ibid., 141.

32. Latrobe, *Impressions Respecting New Orleans*, 21–25.

33. Christovich and Toledano, *Faubourg Tremé and Bayou Road*, 19–24.

34. Irwin, "Portrait of a Neighborhood," 148.

35. Bell, *Revolution, Romanticism, and the Afro-Creole Protest Tradition*, 90; Logsdon and Bell, "Americanization," 319; Desdunes, *Our People and Our History*, 29.

36. Alberts, "Origins."

37. Bell, *Revolution, Romanticism, and the Afro-Creole Protest Tradition*, 148.

38. Alberts, "Origins," 62.

39. Ibid., 66.

40. Bell, *Revolution, Romanticism, and the Afro-Creole Protest Tradition*, 129; http://www.staugustinecatholicchurch-neworleans.org/hist-chron.htm (accessed 17 May 2010).

41. Logsdon and Bell, "Americanization," 234.

42. Tregle, "Creoles and Americans," 152, 156.

43. Logsdon and Bell, "Americanization," 219.

44. Alberts, "Origins," 113, 118; Ochs, "Patriot, a Priest, and a Prelate."

45. Jacobs, "Benevolent Societies," 22; Blassingame, *Black New Orleans*, 147.

46. Logsdon and Bell, "Americanization," 243; Christovich and Toledano, *Faubourg Tremé and Bayou Road*, 105.

47. Blassingame, *Black New Orleans*, 167–68.

48. Latrobe, *Impressions Respecting New Orleans*, 128.

49. Schaffer, *Brass Bands and New Orleans Jazz*.

50. Ibid., 66.

51. Russell, *New Orleans Style*, 217.

52. Ibid.

53. Jerde and Treffinger, *Jazz-Related Sites and Structures*, 292–93.

54. Ibid., 290–93.

55. U.S. Department of the Interior, National Park Service, *New Orleans Jazz Study*, 91.

56. Jerde and Treffinger, *Jazz-Related Sites and Structures*, 289–90.

57. Russell, *New Orleans Style*, 23.

58. Lomax, *Mister Jelly Roll*, 83.

59. Russell, *New Orleans Style*, 105.

60. Ibid., 176–81.

61. Shaik, "Economy Society"; Bryan, "Marcus Christian's Treatment."

CHAPTER 3. THE CLEARANCE FOR HIGH CULTURE

1. Sullivan, "Composers of Color," xxii.

2. Logsdon and Bell, "Americanization," 242; Tregle, "Creoles and Americans," 161, 170; Anthony, "'Lost Boundaries.'"

3. Shaik, "Economy Society," 3.

4. City of New Orleans, Planning and Zoning Commission, *City Plan Report*.

5. Ibid.

6. Ibid., 44.

7. W. H. Wilson, "City Beautiful Movement."

8. Sidney Bezou, interview, 23 September 1982, Friends of the Cabildo Oral History Program, New Orleans Public Library.

9. Ann Kindlesberg, interview, 18 February 1987, Friends of the Cabildo Oral History Program, New Orleans Public Library.

10. "Beauregard Square Selected as Site."

11. Stanonis, *Creating the Big Easy*, 222.

12. Ibid.

13. Ibid.

14. City of New Orleans, Planning and Zoning Commission, *City Plan Report*.

15. Martinez, "Housing Act of 1949."

16. Bellush and Hausknecht, *Urban Renewal*, 3.

17. Haas, *DeLesseps S. Morrison*, 43.

18. Ibid., 73.

19. Harland Bartholomew and Associates, *25-Year Urban Redevelopment Program*, 6.

20. Andre, "Urban Renewal and Housing," 27.

21. Harland Bartholomew and Associates, *Master Plan*, chapter 11, p. 33.

22. "Six City Bond Aims Approved."

23. "Bureau for Six Bond Issues."

24. City of New Orleans, Planning Commission, *Public Buildings Report II*, 30.

25. Ibid., v, 33.

26. M. Smith and Keller, "'Managed Growth,'" 135.

27. Moe and Wilkie, *Changing Places*, 107.

28. City of New Orleans, Planning Commission, *Cultural Center*.

29. Blumenthal, "Urban Journey"; Shepard, "Lincoln Center."

30. Jack Frick to Harold Katner, "Chronology of the Cultural Center," 3 January 1972, New Orleans City Archives.

31. Edward Benjamin to Charles F. O'Doniel, 18 December 1962, New Orleans City Archives.

32. Ott, "Tremé Group."

33. Ott, "Officials Give Tremé Pledge."

34. Charles W. Nutter to Harold Katner, 8 March 1972, John Scales to Harold Katner, 13 April 1972, New Orleans City Archives.

35. Harold Katner to William Rapp, 14 March 1972, New Orleans City Archives.

36. Labouisse, "Ironical History," 76.

CHAPTER 4. KILLING CLAIBORNE'S AVENUE

1. Fullilove, *Root Shock*.

2. Crutcher, "Historical Geographies."

3. Campanella, *Time and Place*, 67.

4. Tregle, "Creoles and Americans," 154.

5. Mosher, Kiem, and Franques, "Downtown Dynamics."

6. Ibid., 506.

7. Ibid., 505.

8. Medley, *We as Freemen*, 16.

9. Long, *Great Southern Babylon*, 138.

10. Widmer, *New Orleans in the Forties*, 184.

11. Anthony, "Negro Creole Community"; Gaudin, "Autocrats and All Saints."

12. Stuart, *Economic Detour*, 3.

13. Brothers, *Louis Armstrong's New Orleans*, 32.

14. *Colored New Orleans*.

15. Samuels, "Remembering North Claiborne"; Plater, "African-American Insurance Enterprises."

16. Samuels, "Remembering North Claiborne," 37.

17. Beito, "Mutual Aid for Social Welfare."

18. *Rhodes Family of Business: Caring for Generations*, http://www.rhodesfuneral.com/rhodes.swf (accessed 5 October 2007).

19. Ingham and Feldman, *African-American Business Leaders*, 178.

20. Samuels, "Remembering North Claiborne," 37.

21. Stuart, *Economic Detour*, 1; *Rhodes Family of Business*.

22. Ibid., 37.

23. Ingham and Feldman, *African-American Business Leaders*, 179.

24. Ibid., 147.

25. Fairclough, *Race and Democracy*, 18–19.

26. Bechet and Blesh, *Treat It Gentle*, 67.

27. Scherman, *Backbeat*, 1.

28. Ibid., 9.

29. Harland Bartholomew and Associates, *Preliminary Report*, 69.

30. Mowbray, *Road to Ruin*, 177.

31. Mohl, "Planned Destruction," 231.

32. Ibid.

33. Ibid.

34. Andrews and Clark, *Arterial Plan for New Orleans*, 5–8.

35. Baumbach and Borah, *Second Battle of New Orleans*, 82.

36. Baumbach and Borah, *Second Battle of New Orleans*, 32; Haas, *DeLesseps S. Morrison*, 43.

37. Samuels, "Remembering North Claiborne," 60.

38. Baumbach and Borah, *Second Battle of New Orleans*, 34–35.

39. Samuels, "Remembering North Claiborne," 65.

40. "51 of 253 Oaks Will Be 'Saved.'"

41. Ibid.

42. Samuels, "Remembering North Claiborne," 78.

43. Ibid.

44. Rose, *Interstate*, 106.

45. Mowbray, *Road to Ruin*, 178.

46. Ibid., 183.

47. *House Divided*.

48. Ibid.

49. Steptoe and Thornton, *Differential Influence*, 60–68.

50. Samuels, "Remembering North Claiborne," 93, 81, 95.

51. Ingham and Feldman, *African-American Business Leaders*, 147.

52. Samuels, "Remembering North Claiborne," 86.

53. Moon, *Interstate Highway System*, 57.

54. Mowbray, *Road to Ruin*, 58.

55. Baumbach and Borah, *Second Battle of New Orleans*, 64–66.

56. Claiborne Avenue Design Team, *CADT I-10 Multi-Use Study*, 18.

57. Ibid.

CHAPTER 5. A PARK FOR LOUIS

1. Crouch, "Louis Armstrong."

2. Morgenstern, *Living*, 61. In 1965, following the passage of major federal civil rights legislation, Armstrong again played in New Orleans.

3. Katz, "Satchmo Tribute Asked."

4. City of New Orleans Public Relations Office, Press Release, 30 June 1972, New Orleans City Archives.

5. Ibid.

6. Ibid.

7. ". . . Proposal Made."

8. Katz, "Armstrong Park Contract Okayed."

9. Edward Benjamin to Planning Commission, 24 June 1973, New Orleans City Archives.

10. Edward Benjamin to Albert Saputo, 6 July 1973, New Orleans City Archives.

11. Edward Benjamin to Albert Saputo, 30 July 1973, Edward Benjamin to Robert Manard, 8 August 1973, New Orleans City Archives.

12. Lafourcade, "Storm of Protest."

13. Eggler, "Park Factions Collide."

14. Omer F. Kuebel to Teddy Gabb, 10 September 1973, Alfred Lozano to Teddy Gabb, 17 September 1973, New Orleans City Archives.

15. Arthur R. Payzant to Patricia Fretwell, 8 September 1973, Donald A. Meyer to Chair, City Planning Commission, 13 September 1973, Betty Wood to City Planning Commission, 1 October 1973, New Orleans City Archives.

16. Ott, "Officials Give Tremé Pledge."

17. Lincoln, "Battle Lines Form."

18. Eggler, "Park Factions Collide."

19. Ibid.

20. Eggler, "Satchmo Park Clears Orleans Planning Panel."

21. Eggler, "Armstrong Park Protests Mount."

22. Joyce Davis, "Tremé Community Funding Rejected."

23. "Armstrong Park Petition Ready."

24. Jack Davis, "Armstrong Park vs. the Automobile."

25. Gormin, "Lagoons OK'd."

26. Ibid.

27. P. Atkinson, "Jazz Event"; P. Atkinson, "Jazz Stars"; Tucker, "Memorial to Satchmo."

28. City of New Orleans, Office of Mayoral Transition, *Special Task Force Report*.

29. Ibid., 9.

30. Ibid., 12.

31. P. Atkinson, "Jazz Stars to Open Armstrong Park."

32. City of New Orleans, Office of Planning and Development, *Bid Proposal*.

33. Harrison Price Company, *Development Feasibility*; Armstrong Park Corporation, *Master Plan*; Dansker and Drew, "Hotels Not Required."

34. Donze, "Developers Spotlight Jazz."

35. Donze, "City Blamed."

36. Donze, "Mayor Setting Pace."

37. "Woman Slain in N.O. Park."

38. Warner, "Armstrong Could Hum Tivoli Tune"; Donze, "Ideas."

39. Tivoli International, *Master Plan*.

40. Economic Consulting Services, *Economic Evaluation of Development*.

41. P. Atkinson, "Jazz Event"; P. Atkinson, "Jazz Stars."

42. Tucker, "Memorial to Satchmo."

43. Frick, "Watchful Neighborhood Surrounds Armstrong Park."

44. "Residents Want Say in Park."

45. Dansker, "Armstrong Offer Should Be Taken."

46. Dansker and Drew, "Hotels Not Required."

47. Donze and Dansker, "Council Rejects Armstrong Plan."

48. Jim Hayes, Morris F. X. Jeff, and Jim Singleton spoke of the effect of personal and political antagonisms between Morial and Barthelemy on discussions regarding Armstrong Park during Morial's tenure as mayor.

49. Akinshiju, "Armstrong Park," 2.

50. Akinshiju, "March Called," 2.

51. Richardson, "Battle for Louis Armstrong Park," 2.

52. Warner, "Money Delay."

53. Warner, "Loan OK'd"; Ruth, "Other Music Ideas."

54. "Paved with Good Intentions"; Frazier and Anderson, "Riverboat Gambling."

55. Eggler, "Tremé Leaders Want Answers."

56. Bridges, "Casino Foe"; Persica, "Once Burned Tremé."

57. "Chronology"; Persica, "Once Burned Tremé."

CHAPTER 6. NATIONAL PARK SAVIOR

1. U.S. Department of the Interior, *National Parks.*

2. City of New Orleans and U.S. Department of the Interior, National Park Service, *Cooperative Agreement.*

3. Eggler, "La. National Park."

4. Ricard, "African-Americans Left Out."

5. Eggler, "La. National Park."

6. M. Smith, "Develop Park," B6.

7. M. Smith, *Economic Development.*

8. G. Roberts, "Movement"; Eggler, "Black Music Museum."

9. Conservation Foundation, *National Parks for the Future.*

10. Ibid., 13.

11. Ibid., 14.

12. U.S. Department of the Interior, *National Parks*, 90.

13. Ibid., 52, 70, 40.

14. U.S. Department of the Interior, National Park Service, *Revision.*

15. Ibid.

16. Machlis, "Usable Knowledge," 45.

17. Ibid., 47.

18. U.S. Department of the Interior, National Park Service, *New Orleans Jazz National Historical Park, Draft General Management Plan*, 118.

19. Preservation of Jazz Advisory Commission Meeting transcript, 3 May 1991, 5–6, Hogan Jazz Archive, Tulane University.

20. U.S. Department of the Interior, National Park Service, *New Orleans Jazz Study,* 73–75.

21. Preservation of Jazz Advisory Commission, Public Hearing Report, 24 August 1991, 122, Hogan Jazz Archive, Tulane University.

22. Ibid., 66.

23. Public Law 103-433, section 1202-b.

24. U.S. Department of the Interior, National Park Service, *New Orleans Jazz National Historical Park, Draft General Management Plan.*

25. Warner, "Morial Draws up Jazz Park Plan"; City of New Orleans, *New Orleans Jazz National Historical Park.*

26. Eggler, "Jazz Park."

27. Stewart, interview.

28. City of New Orleans and U.S. Department of the Interior, National Park Service, *Cooperative Agreement.*

29. U.S. Department of the Interior, National Park Service, *New Orleans Jazz National Historical Park: Final Abbreviated General Management Plan*, 21–47.

30. Louis Armstrong Park is presently locked most of the time, thereby preventing crime from occurring inside its boundaries.

31. University of New Orleans, College of Urban and Public Affairs, *Enhancing the Sense of Place.*

32. During my time as a park ranger, another ranger and I were assigned this specific task.

33. Schroeder and Anderson, "Perception of Personal Safety."

34. McQuaid, "Silent Invader."

35. Harper, interview; White, interview.

36. U.S. Department of the Interior, National Park Service, *New Orleans Jazz National Historical Park, Draft General Management Plan*; U.S. Department of the Interior, National Park Service, *New Orleans Jazz Study.*

37. Hazelwood, interview.

CHAPTER 7. SAVING BLACK TREMÉ

1. Breunlin and Regis, "Putting the Ninth Ward on the Map." The Ninth Ward is located downriver from heart of the city. Its peripheral location fosters a unique community identity in the perceptions both of residents and of outsiders. An outgrowth of that perception is that outsiders are often unfamiliar with the area and thus reluctant to travel there.

2. Route sheets are part of an effective guerrilla advertising strategy that seeks to inform second-line aficionados where they can catch parades. Route sheets are the most reliable way of finding out who is parading and where, as newspapers advertise only the largest anniversary parades and those held for special occasions. The sheets are primarily textual maps that list a parade's starting location, scheduled stops, and end point as well as the participating brass band.

3. Nine Times Social and Pleasure Club, *Coming out the Door.*

4. Borders, "Block Is Hot."

5. Ley, "Rent-Gap"; N. Smith, "Gentrification."

6. The case can be made that the French Quarter gentrified at the same time as or even before the Marigny, but the racial component in the Quarter is not as stated, and the story of gentrification there thus takes on a different tone.

7. Knopp, "Gentrification and Gay Community Development"; Knopp, "Some Theoretical Implications."

8. Cook and Lauria, "Urban Regeneration and Housing."

9. Knopp, "Gentrification and Gay Community Development," 67.

10. Ibid.

11. Kamerick, "Tremé Neighborhood Struggling."

12. Foster, "Rebuilding Esplanade Ridge."

13. LeDoux, interview.

14. Gotham, "Tourism Gentrification."

15. http://www.nps.gov/history/local-law/nhpa1966.htm (accessed 3 May 2007).

16. The register was not started from scratch. Landmarks and buildings already listed in the Historic American Buildings Survey were added to an advisory list to the National Register of Historic Places.

17. http://www.faubourgmarigny.org/historyfmia.htm (accessed 2 March 2007).

18. http://www.prcno.org/aboutprc/mission.php (accessed 2 March 2007).

19. Ibid.

20. Cooper, "Tremé Agency Spending."

21. Cooper, "Aid Office Stands Out"; Cooper, "Armstrong Audit."

22. Cooper, "U.S. Jury Investigates."

23. Sylvain, interview.

24. Cooper, "Blighted Tremé Struggles."

25. Sylvain, interview.

26. Donze, "Council OKs Tremé Historic District."

27. Ibid.

28. Freeman and Braconi, "Gentrification and Displacement."

29. Bolding, *Before and after N. Dorgenois*, 55.

30. Aiges, "Dispute"; Eggler, "Embattled Tremé Community Comes Together."

31. Bostic and Martin, "Black Homeowners," 2447.

32. Ibid.

33. McKenna, "There's No Place Like Home."

34. Preservation Resource Center of New Orleans, http://www.prcno.org./programs/ethnicheritage.php.

35. Borders "Block Is Hot."

36. LaCoste, "Battling Blight."

37. Kamerick, "Tremé Neighborhood Struggling."

38. Hearing of the Preservation of Jazz Advisory Commission, 24 August 1991, 25 June 1992, Hogan Jazz Archive, Tulane University.

39. Hearing of the Preservation of Jazz Advisory Commission, 25 June 1992, Hogan Jazz Archive, Tulane University.

40. "NIGGERS FOR SALE CHEAP — IN TREMÉ," spring 1993, Hogan Jazz Archive, Tulane University.

EPILOGUE

1. Reckdahl, "St. Joseph's Night Gone Blue"; Elie, "Indian Relations Strained."

2. Author's notes.

3. Perlstein, "Chief of Chiefs."

4. Babbitt, "Make It an Island"; Colten, "Restore the Marsh"; Petroski, "Raise the Ground."

5. Crutcher, "Build Diversity."

6. City of New Orleans, Bring New Orleans Back Commission, *Report*, 17–22.

7. Regis, "Second-Line Parades"; Reckdahl, "Price of Parading"; Simmons, "New Orleans' Fees."

8. Carol Kolinshack and Katie Schwartzman, "Police Escort Fees for First Amendment Activity," American Civil Liberties Union to Warren Riley, 16 May 2006, author's files.

9. Eaton, "In Storm's Aftermath"; Nolan, "St. Augustine Parish to Close"; Nolan, "Archdiocese Closes Seven Churches"; M. Roberts, "Archdiocese of New Orleans."

10. Pastoral Council of St. Augustine Parish to Alfred Hughes, 14 March 2006, 20 March 2006, author's files.

11. Pastoral Council of St. Augustine Parish to Alfred Hughes, 24 March 2006, author's files.

12. Nolan, "Archbishop Closes St. Augustine"; Nolan, "Supporters Still in Church"; *Shake the Devil Off.*

13. Nolan, "Parish Gets Chance"; Nolan, "St. Augustine Parish Counts Its Blessings."

14. Hanlon, "Success by Design."

15. Varney, "HANO Wants."

16. Quigley, "New Orleans"; Quigley, "Tale of Two Sisters"; Quigley, "Bulldozing Hope."

17. O'Reilly and Crutcher, "Parallel Politics," 259.

18. "Police Must Patrol"; Ussery, "Rampart Shooting Victim Is Dead."

19. Eggler, "4 More Pieces."

20. Peck, "Vieux Redo"; Eggler, "Condos Get Green Light"; Thomas, "Grand Visions."

21. Varney, "Unlicensed N. Rampart Clubs."

22. Grove, "Rampart Festival"; Grove, "Friends of North Rampart"; Kemp, "Armstrong Park"; Grove, "North Rampart Street Salutes Satchmo"; Dungca, "North Rampart Renaissance."

23. Ramsey, "North Rampart Needs a Savior," 8.

BIBLIOGRAPHY

MANUSCRIPT SOURCES

Amistad Research Center, Tulane University
Harland Bartholomew and Associates Collection, Washington University
Hermon Dunlap Smith Center for the History of Cartography, Newberry Library
Hogan Jazz Archive, Tulane University
Louisiana and Special Collections, Earl K. Long Library, University of New Orleans
Louisiana and Special Collections, Howard-Tilton Library, Tulane University
Louisiana Division and Special Collections, New Orleans Library
New Orleans City Archives
Special Collections, Washington University
Williams Research Center, Historic New Orleans Collection

INTERVIEWS

Carl Galmon, 9 September 1999
Rayford Harper, 23 September 1996
James Hayes, 10 September 1999
Gayle Hazelwood, 1 March 2000
Dr. Morris F. X. Jeff Jr., 11 June 2002
Father Jerome LeDoux, 15 June 2005
James Singleton, 10 June 2002
Jack Stewart, 3 October 1999
Vincent Sylvain, 10 October 1999
Robin White, 23 September 1996

SECONDARY SOURCES

Books

Barker, Danny. *A Life in Jazz*. New York: Oxford University Press, 1986.
Barker, Danny, and Alyn Shipton. *Buddy Bolden and the Last Days of Storyville*. New York: Cassell, 1998.
Baumbach, Richard, and William Borah. *The Second Battle of New Orleans: A History of the Vieux Carré Riverfront Expressway Controversy*. Tuscaloosa: University of Alabama Press, 1981.

Bechet, Sidney, and Rudi Blesh. *Treat It Gentle: An Autobiography*. New York: Da Capo, 1978.

Bell, Caryn. *Revolution, Romanticism, and the Afro-Creole Protest Tradition in Louisiana, 1718–1868*. Baton Rouge: Louisiana State University Press, 1997.

Bellush, Jewell, and Murray Hausknecht, eds. *Urban Renewal: People, Politics, and Planning*. Garden City, N.Y.: Doubleday, 1967.

Berry, Jason, Jonathan Foose, and Tad Jones. *Up from the Cradle of Jazz: New Orleans Music since World War II*. New York: Da Capo, 1986.

Blassingame, John. *Black New Orleans, 1869–1880*. Chicago: University of Chicago Press, 1973.

Bolding, Ebony. *Before and after N. Dorgenois*. New Orleans: Soft Skull, 2005.

Boyer, Christine. *Dreaming the Rational City*. Cambridge: MIT Press, 1983.

Breunlin, Rachel, Abram Himelstein, and Bethany Rogers. *Cornerstones: Celebrating the Everyday Monuments and Gathering Places of New Orleans*. New Orleans: UNO Press, 2008.

Brothers, Thomas David. *Louis Armstrong's New Orleans*. New York: Norton, 2006.

Broyard, Bliss. *One Drop: My Father's Hidden Life — A Story of Race and Family Secrets*. New York: Little, Brown, 2007.

Buerkle, Jack, and Danny Barker. *Bourbon Street Black: The New Orleans Black Jazzman*. New York: Oxford University Press, 1973.

Calhoun, Craig, ed. *Habermas and the Public Sphere*. Cambridge: MIT Press.

Campanella, Richard. *Geographies of New Orleans: Urban Fabrics before the Storm*. Lafayette: Center for Louisiana Studies, 2006.

——. *Time and Place in New Orleans: Past Geographies in the Present Day*. Gretna, La.: Pelican, 2002.

Campanella, Richard, and Marina Campanella. *New Orleans Then and Now*. Gretna, La.: Pelican, 1999.

Castells, Manuel. *The City and the Grassroots: A Cross-Cultural Theory of Urban Social Movements*. Berkeley: University of California Press, 1983.

Christovich, Mary, and Roulhac Toledano. *Faubourg Tremé and Bayou Road*. Vol. 6 of *New Orleans Architecture*. Gretna, La.: Pelican, 1980.

Cohn, Nik. *Triksta: Life and Death and New Orleans Rap*. New York: Knopf, 2005.

Collins, R. *New Orleans Jazz: A Revised History*. New York: Vantage, 1996.

Colored New Orleans: High Points of Negro Endeavor. New Orleans: Colored Civic League of New Orleans, 1922–23.

Colten, Craig E. *An Unnatural Metropolis: Wresting New Orleans from Nature*. Baton Rouge: Louisiana State University Press, 2005.

Desdunes, Rodolphe. *Our People and Our History*. Baton Rouge: Louisiana State University Press, 1911.

Dominguez, Virginia. *White by Definition*. New Brunswick: Rutgers University Press, 1986.

Downs, Tom. *Lonely Planet New Orleans*. Oakland, Calif.: Lonely Planet, 2006.

Drake, Sinclair. *Black Metropolis: A Study of Negro Life in a Northern City*. New York: Harcourt, Brace, 1945.

Duncan, Jim, and Nancy Duncan. *Landscapes of Privilege: Politics of the Aesthetic in an American Suburb*. New York: Routledge, 2003.

Fainstein, Susan, Norman Fainstein, Richard Hill, Dennis Judd, and Michael Smith, eds. *Restructuring the City: The Political Economy of Urban Redevelopment*. New York: Longman, 1983.

Fairclough, Adam. *Race and Democracy: The Civil Rights Struggle in Louisiana, 1915–1972*. Athens: University of Georgia Press, 1995.

Fodor's New Orleans 2007. New York: Fodor's, 2006.

Freund, David. *Colored Property: State Policy and White Racial Politics in Suburban America*. Chicago: University Of Chicago Press, 2007.

Fullilove, Mindy. *Root Shock: How Tearing up City Neighborhoods Hurts America, and What We Can Do About It*. New York: Ballantine, 2004.

Germany, Kent. *New Orleans after the Promises: Poverty, Citizenship, and the Search for the Great Society*. Athens: University of Georgia Press, 2007.

Goings, K. W., and R. A. Mohl, eds. *The New African American Urban History*. Thousand Oaks, Calif.: Sage, 1996.

Gotham, Kevin Fox. *Authentic New Orleans: Tourism, Culture, and Race in the Big Easy*. New York: New York University Press, 2007.

Haas, Edward. *DeLesseps S. Morrison and the Image of Reform: New Orleans Politics, 1946–1961*. Baton Rouge: Louisiana State University Press, 1974.

Habermas, Jürgen. *The Structural Transformation of the Public Sphere: An Inquiry into a Category of Bourgeois Society*. Cambridge: Polity, 1989.

Hall, Gwendolyn Midlo. *Africans in Colonial Louisiana: The Development of Afro-Creole Culture in the Eighteenth Century*. Baton Rouge: Louisiana State University Press, 1992.

Hanger, Kimberly S. *Bounded Lives, Bounded Places: Free Black Society in Colonial New Orleans, 1769–1803*. Durham: Duke University Press, 1997.

Harvey, David. *The Condition of Postmodernity: An Enquiry into the Origins of Social Change*. Oxford: Blackwell, 1989.

Hayden, Delores. *The Power of Place: Urban Landscapes as Public History*. Cambridge: MIT Press, 1995.

Haymes, Stephen. *Race, Culture, and City: A Pedagogy for Black Urban Struggle*. Albany: State University of New York Press, 1995.

Herczog, Mary. *Frommer's New Orleans 2007*. Hoboken, N.J.: Wiley, 2007.

Hirsch, Arnold. *Making the Second Ghetto: Race and Housing in Chicago, 1940–1960*. New York: Cambridge University Press, 1983.

Hirsch, Arnold, and Joseph Logsdon. *Creole New Orleans: Race and Americanization*. Baton Rouge: Louisiana State University Press, 1992.

hooks, bell. *Yearning: Race, Gender, and Cultural Politics*. Boston: South End, 1990.

hooks, bell, and Cornel West. *Breaking Bread: Insurgent Black Intellectual Life*. Boston: South End, 1991.

Ingersoll, Thomas. "A View from the Parish Jail: New Orleans." *Common-Place* 3, no. 4. http://www.common-place.org/vol-03/no-04/new-orleans/ (accessed 5 May 2010).

Ingham, John N., and Lynne B. Feldman. *African-American Business Leaders: A Biographical Dictionary*. Westport, Conn.: Greenwood, 1994.

Irvin, Hilary Somerville. *Vieux Carré Commission History*. http://www.cityofno.com/pg-59-12-history — news.aspx (accessed 8 June 2010).

Kein, Sybil, ed. *Creole: The History and Legacy of Louisiana's Free People of Color*. Baton Rouge: Louisiana State University Press, 2000.

———. *Gumbo People*. New Orleans: Margaret Media, 1999.

Kirsch, Elise. *"Down-Town" New Orleans in the Early "Eighties": Customs and Characters of Old Robertson Street and Its Neighborhood*. New Orleans: n.p., 1951.

Knox, Paul, ed. *The Restless Urban Landscape*. Englewood Cliffs, N.J.: Prentice Hall, 1993.

———. *Urbanization*. Englewood Cliffs, N.J.: Prentice Hall, 1994.

Kostof, Spiro. *The City Assembled: Elements of Urban Form through History*. Boston: Bulfinch, 1994.

Latrobe, Benjamin H. *Impressions Respecting New Orleans*. Edited by Samuel Wilson Jr. New York: Columbia University Press, 1951.

Lefebvre, Henri. *The Production of Space*. Cambridge: Blackwell, 1991.

Lewis, Peirce. *New Orleans: The Making of an Urban Landscape*. Cambridge: Ballinger, 1976.

———. *New Orleans: The Making of an Urban Landscape*. 2nd ed. Santa Fe, N.M.: Center for American Places, 2003.

Lomax, Alan. *Mister Jelly Roll: The Fortunes of Jelly Roll Morton, New Orleans Creole and "Inventor of Jazz."* New York: Duell, Sloan, and Pearce, 1950.

Long, Alecia. *The Great Southern Babylon: Sex, Race, and Respectability in New Orleans, 1865–1920*. Baton Rouge: Louisiana State University Press, 2004.

Medley, Keith Weldon. *We as Freemen: Plessy v. Ferguson*. Gretna, La.: Pelican, 2003.

Moe, Richard, and Carter Wilkie. *Changing Places: Rebuilding Community in the Age of Sprawl*. New York: Holt, 1997.

Moon, Henry. *The Interstate Highway System*. Washington, D.C.: Association of American Geographers, 1994.

Morgenstern, Dan. *Living with Jazz*. New York: Pantheon, 2004.

Mowbray, A. Q. *Road to Ruin*. Philadelphia: Lippincott, 1969.

Nelson, Ashley. *The Combination*. New Orleans: Soft Skull, 2005.

Nine Times Social and Pleasure Club. *Coming out the Door for the Ninth Ward*. New Orleans: Neighborhood Story Project, 2006.

Rabinowitz, Howard. *Race Relations in the Urban South*. Athens: University of Georgia Press, 1996.

Roach, Joseph. *Cities of the Dead*. New York: Columbia University Press, 1996.

Rose, M. *Interstate: Express Highway Politics, 1939–1989*. Knoxville: University of Tennessee Press, 1990.

Russell, Bill. *New Orleans Style*. New Orleans: Jazzology, 1994.

Schaffer, William. *Brass Bands and New Orleans Jazz*. Baton Rouge: Louisiana State University Press, 1977.

Schein, Richard, ed. *Landscape and Race in the United States*. New York: Routledge, 2006.

Scherman, Tony. *Backbeat: Earl Palmer's Story*. Washington, D.C.: Smithsonian Institution, 1999.

Smith, Michael. *Mardi Gras Indians*. Gretna, La.: Pelican, 1994.

Soja, Edward. *Postmodern Geographies: The Reassertion of Space in Critical Social Theory*. London: Verso, 1989.

Sorkin, Michael, ed. *Variations on a Theme Park: The New American City and the End of Public Space*. New York: Hill and Wang, 1992.

Squires, Gregory, ed. *Unequal Partnerships: The Political Economy of Urban Redevelopment in Postwar America*. New Brunswick: Rutgers University Press, 1989.

Stanonis, Anthony J. *Creating the Big Easy: New Orleans and the Emergence of Modern Tourism, 1918–1945*. Athens: University of Georgia Press, 2006.

Steinberg, Phil, and Rob Shields. *What Is a City?: Rethinking the Urban after Hurricane Katrina*. Athens: University of Georgia Press, 2008.

Stuart, Merah. *An Economic Detour: A History of Insurance in the Lives of American Negroes*. College Park, Md.: McGrath, 1969.

Sublette, Ned. *The World That Made New Orleans: From Spanish Silver to Congo Square*. Chicago: Hill, 2008.

Wagner, Fritz, Timothy Joder, and Anthony Mumphrey, eds. *Urban Revitalization: Policies and Programs*. Thousand Oaks, Calif.: Sage, 1994.

Widmer, Mary. *New Orleans in the Forties*. Gretna, La.: Pelican, 1990.

Wiese, Andrew. *Places of Their Own: African American Suburbanization in the Twentieth Century*. Chicago: University of Chicago Press, 2005.

Wilson, Chris, and Paul Groth, eds. *Everyday America: Cultural Landscape Studies after J. B. Jackson*. Berkeley: University of California Press, 2003.

Wilson, William H. *The City Beautiful Movement*. Baltimore: Johns Hopkins University Press, 1994.

Zukin, Sharon. *The Culture of Cities*. Cambridge: Blackwell, 1995.

Journal Articles and Book Chapters

Anthony, Arthé A. "'Lost Boundaries': Racial Passing and Poverty in Segregated New Orleans." *Louisiana History* 36, no. 3 (1995): 291–312.

Atkinson, Connie. "Whose New Orleans?: Music's Place in the Packaging of New

Orleans for Tourism." In *Tourists and Tourism*, edited by Simone Abram, Jacqueline Waldren, and Donald Macleod. New York: Oxford University Press, 1997.

Barthelemy, Anthony G. "Light, Bright, Damn Near White: Race, the Politics of Genealogy, and the Strange Case of Susie Guilory." In *Creole: The History and Legacy of Louisiana's Free People of Color*, edited by Sybil Kein. Baton Rouge: Louisiana State University Press, 2000.

Beito, David. "Mutual Aid for Social Welfare: The Case of American Fraternal Societies." *Critical Review* 4, no. 4 (1990): 709–36.

Bellush, Jewell, and Murray Hausknecht. "Urban Renewal: An Historical Overview." In *Urban Renewal: People, Politics, and Planning*, edited by Jewell Bellush and Murray Hausknecht. Garden City, N.Y.: Doubleday, 1967.

Blassingame, John. "Before the Ghetto: The Making of the Black Community in Savannah Georgia, 1865–1880." *Journal of Social History* 6, no. 4 (1973): 463–88.

Bostic, Raphael, and Richard Martin. "Black Homeowners as a Gentrifying Force?: Neighborhood Dynamics in the Context of Minority Home-Ownership." *Urban Studies* 40, no. 12 (2003): 2427–49.

Boxer, Sarah. "Herriman: Cartoonist Who Equalled Cervantes." Telegraph.co.uk, 7 July 2007 (accessed 5 May 2010).

Boyer, Christine. "The City of Illusion: New York's Public Places." In *The Restless Urban Landscape*, edited by Paul Knox. Englewood Cliffs, N.J.: Prentice Hall, 1993.

Breunlin, Rachel, and Helen Regis. "Putting the Ninth Ward on the Map: Race, Place, and Transformation in Desire, New Orleans." *American Anthropologist* 108, no. 4 (2006): 744–64.

Brooks, Jane, Teresa Wilkerson, and Alma Young. "The Jackson Brewery: Resolving Land Use Change in a Cooperative Mode." *Urban Land* 43, no. 6 (1984): 20–25.

Brooks, Jane, and Alma Young. "Revitalizing the Central Business District in the Face of Decline: The Case of New Orleans, 1973–1993." *Town Planning Review* 64, no. 3 (1993): 251–71.

Brown, Elsa Barkley, and Gregg Kimball. "Mapping the Terrain of Black Richmond." In *The New African American Urban History*, edited by K. W. Goings and R. A. Mohl. Thousand Oaks, Calif.: Sage, 1996.

Bryan, Violet H. "Marcus Christian's Treatment of Les Gens de Couleur Libre." In *Creole: The History and Legacy of Louisiana's Free People of Color*, edited by Sybil Kein. Baton Rouge: Louisiana State University Press, 2000.

Cook, Christine, and Mickey Lauria. "Urban Regeneration and Housing in New Orleans." *Urban Affairs Review* 30, no. 4 (1995): 538–57.

Crutcher, Michael. "Historical Geographies of Race in a New Orleans Afro-Creole Landscape." In *Landscape and Race in the United States*, edited by Richard H. Schein. New York: Routledge, 2006.

Dunbar-Nelson, Alice. "People of Color in Louisiana." Pts. 1 and 2. *Journal of Negro History* 1, no. 4 (1916): 361–76; 2, no. 1 (1917): 51–78.

Fraser, Nancy. "Rethinking the Public Sphere: A Contribution to the Critique of Actually Existing Democracy." *Social Text* 25–26 (1990): 56–80.

Freeman, Lance, and Frank Braconi. "Gentrification and Displacement." *Urban Prospect* 8, no. 1 (2002): 1–4.

Gotham, Kevin Fox. "Tourism Gentrification: The Case of New Orleans' Vieux Carre (French Quarter)." *Urban Studies* 42, no. 7 (2005): 1099–1121.

Groth, Paul, and Chris Wilson. "The Polyphony of Cultural Landscape Study: An Introduction." In *Everyday America: Cultural Landscape Studies after J. B. Jackson*, edited by Chris Wilson and Paul Groth. Berkeley: University of California Press, 2003.

Hanlon, James. "Success by Design: HOPE VI, New Urbanism, and the Neoliberal Transformation of Public Housing in the United States." *Environment and Planning A* 42, no. 1 (2010): 80–98.

Hirsch, Arnold. "Simply a Matter of Black and White." In *Creole New Orleans*, edited by Arnold Hirsch and Joseph Logsdon. Baton Rouge: Louisiana State University Press, 1992.

Jacobs, Claude F. "Benevolent Societies of Black New Orleans during the Late Nineteenth and Early Twentieth Centuries." *Louisiana History* 29, no. 1 (Winter 1988): 21–33.

Johnson, Jerah. "Colonial New Orleans: A Fragment of the Eighteenth-Century French Ethos." In *Creole New Orleans*, edited by Arnold Hirsch and Joseph Logsdon. Baton Rouge: Louisiana State University Press, 1992.

———. "New Orleans's Congo Square: An Urban Setting for Early Afro-American Culture Formation." *Louisiana History* 32, no. 2 (1991): 117–57.

Kmen, Henry. "The Roots of Jazz and Dance in the Place Congo: A Re-Appraisal." *Inter-American Musical Research Yearbook* 8 (1972): 5–16.

Knopp, Lawrence. "Some Theoretical Implications of Gay Involvement in an Urban Land Market." *Political Geography Quarterly* 9, no. 4 (1990): 337–52.

Lachance, Paul F. "The 1809 Immigration of Saint-Domingue Refugees to New Orleans: Reception, Integration, and Impact." *Louisiana History* 29, no. 2 (1988): 109–41.

Lauria, Mickey, Robert Whelan, and Alma Young. "Revitalization of New Orleans." In *Urban Revitalization: Policies and Programs*, edited by Fritz Wagner, Timothy Joder, and Anthony Mumphrey. Thousand Oaks, Calif.: Sage, 1994.

Lewis, Earl. "Connecting Memory, Self, and the Power of Place in African American Urban History." In *The New African American Urban History*, edited by K. W. Goings and R. A. Mohl. Thousand Oaks, Calif.: Sage, 1996.

Ley, David. "The Rent-Gap Revisited." *Annals of the Association of American Geographers* 77, no. 3 (1987): 465–68.

Logsdon, Joseph, and Caryn Bell. "Americanization of New Orleans, 1850–1900." In *Creole New Orleans*, edited by Arnold Hirsch and Joseph Logsdon. Baton Rouge: Louisiana State University Press, 1992.

Machlis, Gary. "Usable Knowledge: A Progress Report on the NPS Social Science Program." *Park Science* 20, no. 1 (2000): 45–47.

Marquis, D. "The New Orleans Jazz Funeral." *Second Line* 54, no. 1 (Spring 1999).

Martin, Joan M. "*Plaçage* and the Louisiana *Gens De Couleur Libre.*" In *Creole: The History and Legacy of Louisiana's Free People of Color*, edited by Sybil Kein. Baton Rouge: Louisiana State University Press, 2000.

Martinez, Silvia. "The Housing Act of 1949: Its Place in the Realization of the American Dream of Homeownership." *Housing Policy Debate*, 11, no. 2 (2000). http://www.innovations.harvard.edu/showdoc.html?id=3043 (accessed 5 November 2009).

Mitchell, Don. "The End of Public Space?: People's Park, Definitions of the Public, and Democracy." *Annals of the Association of American Geographers* 85 (1995): 109–33.

———. "Introduction: Public Space and the City." *Urban Geography* 17, no. 3 (1996): 127–31.

———. "Political Violence, Order, and the Legal Construction of Public Space: Power and the Public Forum." *Urban Geography* 17, no. 2 (1996): 152–78.

Mohl, Raymond A. "Planned Destruction: The Interstates and Central City Housing." In *From Tenements to the Taylor Homes: In Search of an Urban Housing Policy in Twentieth-Century America*, edited by Roger Biles, John Bauman, and Kristin Szylvian. University Park: Pennsylvania State University Press, 2000.

———. "Race and Space in the Modern City: Interstate 95 and the Black Community in Miami." In *Urban Policy in Twentieth-Century America*, edited by Arnold Hirsch and Raymond Mohl. New Brunswick: Rutgers University Press, 1993.

Mosher, Anne, Barry Kiem, and Susan Franques. "Downtown Dynamics." *Geographical Review* 85, no. 4 (1995): 497–517.

Mumphrey, Anthony, and Pamela Moomau. "New Orleans: An Island in the Sunbelt." *Public Administration Quarterly* 8, no. 1 (1984): 91–111.

O'Reilly, Kathleen, and Michael Crutcher. "Parallel Politics: The Spatial Power of New Orleans's Labor Day Parades." *Social and Cultural Geography* 7, no. 2 (2006): 245–65.

Ochs, Stephen J. "A Patriot, a Priest, and a Prelate: Black Catholic Activism in Civil War New Orleans." *U.S. Catholic Historian*, 12, no. 1 (1994): 49–75.

Plater, Michael. "African-American Insurance Enterprises: An Early Vehicle for Economic and Social Development." *Journal of Management History* 3, no. 1 (1997): 42–58.

Regis, Helen. "Blackness and the Politics of Memory in the New Orleans Second Line." *American Ethnologist* 28, no. 4 (2000): 752–77.

———. "Second-Line Parades, Citizenship and the Future of Public Space in New Orleans after Katrina." In *Espaces Précaires: Énonciation des Lieux/Le Lieu de l'énonciation dans les Contextes Francophones Interculturels*, edited by Adelaide Russo and Simon Harel. Saint Nicholas, Quebec: Presses de l'Université Laval, forthcoming.

———. "Second Lines, Minstrelsy, and the Contested Landscape of New Orleans Afro-Creole Festivals." *Cultural Anthropology* 14, no. 4 (1999): 472–504.

Ruddick, Susan. "Constructing Difference in Public Spaces: Race, Class, and Gender as Interlocking Systems." *Urban Geography* 17, no. 2 (1996): 132–51.

Schroeder, Herbert W., and L. M. Anderson. "Perception of Personal Safety in Urban Recreation Sites." *Journal of Leisure Research* 16, no. 2 (1984): 178–94.

Shaik, Fatima. "The Economy Society and Community Support for Jazz." *Jazz Archivist* 18 (2004): 1–9.

Smith, Michael P., and Marlene Keller. "'Managed Growth' and the Politics of Uneven Development in New Orleans." In *Restructuring the City: The Political Economy of Urban Redevelopment*, edited by Susan Fainstein, Norman Fainstein, Richard Hill, Dennis Judd, and Michael Smith. New York: Longman, 1983.

Smith, Neil. "Gentrification and the Rent-Gap." *Annals of the Association of American Geographers* 77, no. 3 (1987): 462–65.

———. "New City, New Frontier: The Lower East Side as Wild, Wild West." In *Variations on a Theme Park*, edited by Michael Sorkin. New York: Hill and Wang, 1992.

Staeheli, Lynn, and Albert Thompson. "Community, Citizenship, and Struggles for Public Space." *Professional Geographer* 49, no. 1 (1997): 28–38.

Sullivan, Lester. "Composers of Color of Nineteenth Century New Orleans." In *Creole: The History and Legacy of Louisiana's Free People of Color*, edited by Sybil Kein. Baton Rouge: Louisiana State University Press, 2000.

Tregle, Joseph. "Creoles and Americans." In *Creole New Orleans*, edited by Arnold Hirsch and Joseph Logsdon. Baton Rouge: Louisiana State University Press, 1992.

Vander Steop, G. "Interpretive Facilities: Like Oil and Water?" *Legacy*, January–February 1999, 21–25.

Whelan, Robert. "New Orleans: Public-Private Partnerships and Uneven Development." In *Unequal Partnerships: The Political Economy of Urban Redevelopment in Postwar America*, edited by Gregory Squires. New Brunswick: Rutgers University Press, 1989.

Whelan, Robert, Alma Young, and Mickey Lauria. "Urban Regimes in New Orleans." *Journal of Urban Affairs* 16, no. 1 (1994): 1–21.

White, Shane. "'It Was a Proud Day': African Americans, Festivals, and Parades in the North, 1741–1834." In *The New African American Urban History*, edited by K. W. Goings and R. A. Mohl. Thousand Oaks, Calif.: Sage, 1996.

Young, Alma. "Urban Development Action Grants: The New Orleans Experience." *Public Affairs Quarterly* 8, no. 1 (1984): 112–29.

Newspaper and Magazine Articles

Aiges, S. "Dispute over Live Music Pits Bar Owners and Residents." *New Orleans Times-Picayune*, 24 March 1993.

Akinshiju, O. "Armstrong Park: What's Really Going On . . . ." *Louisiana Data News Weekly*, 24 March 1990.

——. "March Called to Protest Armstrong Development." *Louisiana Data News Weekly*, 31 March 1990.

"Armstrong Park Petition Ready." *New Orleans Times-Picayune*, 24 March 1976.

Atkinson, P. "Jazz Event to Dedicate Park." *New Orleans Times-Picayune*, 8 March 1980, sec. 5, p. 1.

——. "Jazz Stars to Open Armstrong Park." *New Orleans Times-Picayune*, 1 April 1980.

Babbitt, Bruce. "Make It an Island." *New York Times*, 10 September 2005.

Beaulieu, L. "Tremé Leader: Park to Hurt Poor Blacks." *New Orleans Times-Picayune*, 11 March 1983.

"Beauregard Square Selected as Site." *New Orleans Times-Picayune*, 12 April 1928.

Berry, J. "Noble Warriors." *New Orleans Gambit Weekly*, 6 December 1990.

Blumenthal, Ralph. "An Urban Journey from Slum to Cultural Acropolis." *New York Times*, 1 June 1999.

Borders, J. B. "The Block Is Hot: Adolph and Naydja Bynum Have Transformed a Sliver of New Orleans into a Charming Haven." *Uptown*, 22 January 2008. http://uptownmagazine.com/2008/01/new-orleans-real-estate-bynums/. (accessed 8 June 2010).

Bridges, Tyler. "Casino Foe Says Neighborhood Should Cash in Nonetheless." *New Orleans Times-Picayune*, 4 October 1993.

"Bureau for Six Bond Issues." *New Orleans Times-Picayune*, 8 February 1959.

Carter, T. "Measure What We've Lost." *New Orleans Times-Picayune*, 13 April 1997.

"Claiborne Fixings." *New Orleans Times-Picayune*, 15 November 1961.

"Chronology." *Baton Rouge Advocate*, 23 November 1995.

Colten, Craig E. "Restore the Marsh." *New York Times*, 10 September 2005.

Cooper, C. "Aid Office Stands Out in Low-Rent District." *New Orleans Times-Picayune*, 13 February 1994.

——. "Armstrong Audit Shows Abuses." *New Orleans Times-Picayune*, 26 July 1994.

——. "Blighted Tremé Struggles to Regain Historic Status; City Renovation Sparks Rebirth." *New Orleans Times-Picayune*, 24 November 1997.

——. "Tremé Agency Spending Attacked." *New Orleans Times-Picayune*, 10 October 1997.

——. "U.S. Jury Investigates Files of Treme Housing Agency." *New Orleans Times-Picayune*, 21 August 1997.

Crouch, Stanley. "Louis Armstrong." *Time Magazine*, 8 June 1998, 157.

Crutcher, Michael. "Build Diversity." *New York Times*, 10 September 2005.

"Cuban Refugees Arrive Destitute." *La Gazette*, 6 June 1809, 3.

Dansker, B. "Armstrong Offer Should Be Taken, Committee Says." *New Orleans Times-Picayune*, 21 September 1983.

——— . "Plans for Armstrong Park Fought." *New Orleans Times-Picayune*, 23 July 1983.

Dansker, B., and B. Drew. "Hotels Not Required of Armstrong Park Developer, City Says." *New Orleans Times-Picayune*, 26 March 1983.

Davis, Jack. "Armstrong Park vs. the Automobile." *New Orleans States-Item*, 24 March 1976.

Davis, Joyce. "Tremé Community Funding Rejected." *New Orleans Times-Picayune*, 31 December 1974.

Donze, F. "Armstrong Park Redevelopment Foes Want Plan Dropped." *New Orleans Times-Picayune*, 2 March 1990.

——— . "City Blamed for Park's Problems." *New Orleans Times-Picayune*, 15 January 1987.

——— . "Council OKs Tremé Historic District." *New Orleans Times-Picayune*, 7 October 1998.

——— . "Developers Spotlight Jazz in Armstrong Park Plan." *New Orleans Times-Picayune*, 5 April 1984.

——— . "Ideas up against a Record of Failures." *New Orleans Times-Picayune*, 16 October 1987.

——— . "Mayor Setting Pace to Jazz up Armstrong Park." *New Orleans Times-Picayune*, 11 April 1987.

Donze, F., and B. Dansker. "Council Rejects Armstrong Plan, Raises Morial's Salary to $75,905." *New Orleans Times-Picayune*, 2 December 1983.

Dungca, Nicole. "North Rampart Renaissance: Citizens and Business Owners Are Determined to Change the Face — and the Fate — of a Once-Thriving Corridor." *New Orleans Times-Picayune*, 19 September 2008.

Eaton, Leslie. "In Storm's Aftermath, Catholics Retrench." *New York Times*, 10 February 2006.

Eggler, Bruce. "4 More Pieces Fit Master Plan Puzzle: North Rampart Seen as Arts, Cultural Area." *New Orleans Times-Picayune*, 23 October 2002.

——— . "Armstrong Park Protests Mount." *New Orleans States-Item*, 8 November 1973.

——— . "Black Music Museum Gets Council Approval." *New Orleans Times-Picayune*, 22 April 1994.

——— . "Condos Get Green Light on Rampart: Council OKs Waivers for 'Classic Building.'" *New Orleans Times-Picayune*, 11 February 2005.

——— . "Convention Center Weighs Expansion." *New Orleans Times-Picayune*, 26 September 1999.

——— . "Embattled Tremé Community Comes Together." *New Orleans Times-Picayune*, 21 November 1994.

——— . "Jazz Center Plan Gains Support." *New Orleans Times-Picayune*, 28 July 1990.

——— . "Jazz Park Faces Money Snag as Panel Gears Up." *New Orleans Times-Picayune*, 26 January 1996.

——— . "La. National Park Outgrows Its Name." *New Orleans Times-Picayune*, 26 March 1990.

———. "Park Factions Collide." *New Orleans States-Item*, 13 September 1973.

———. "Satchmo Park Clears Orleans Planning Panel." *New Orleans States-Item*, 18 October 1973.

———. "Satchmo Park Work to Start." *New Orleans States-Item*, 11 April 1974.

———. "Tremé Leaders Want Answers before Supporting Casino Site." *New Orleans Times-Picayune*, 4 June 1993.

———. "Tribute to Satchmo? Park Factions Collide." *New Orleans States-Item*, 1 September 1973.

Elie, Lolis E. "Indian Relations Strained." *New Orleans Times-Picayune*, 23 March 2005.

"51 of 253 Oaks Will Be 'Saved.'" *New Orleans Times-Picayune*, 15 November 1961.

Foster, M. "Rebuilding Esplanade Ridge." *New Orleans Times-Picayune*, 29 January 2000.

Frazier, Lisa, and Ed Anderson. "Riverboat Gambling Goes to Roemer." *New Orleans Times-Picayune*, 9 July 1991.

Frick, Kathleen. "Watchful Neighborhood Surrounds Armstrong Park." *New Orleans Times-Picayune/States-Item*, 17 August 1980.

Gormin, Patricia. "Lagoons OK'd — With Parking Compromise." *New Orleans Times-Picayune*, 26 March 1976.

Grove, Roberta. "Friends of North Rampart Tunes into Satchmo." *New Orleans Times-Picayune*, 9 August 2007.

———. "North Rampart Street Salutes Satchmo." *New Orleans Times-Picayune*, 7 August 2008.

———. "Rampart Festival Stirs up Pride of Place." *New Orleans Times-Picayune*, 29 November 2007.

"Jazz Stars to Open Armstrong Park." *New Orleans Times-Picayune*, 1 April 1980, sec. 3.

Jupiter, Clare. "Armstrong Park: Happy Birthday?" *New Orleans States-Item*, 21 January 1975.

Kamerick, Megan. "Tremé Neighborhood Struggling with Gentrification, Crime." *New Orleans CityBusiness*, 24 June 2002. http://findarticles.com/p/articles/mi_qn4200/is_20020624/ai_n10172531/?tag=content;col1 (accessed 1 July 2002).

Katz, A. "Armstrong Park Contract Okayed." *New Orleans States-Item*, 6 April 1973.

———. "Satchmo Tribute Asked." *New Orleans States-Item*, 30 June 1972.

Kemp, Jon. "Armstrong Park Hosting North Rampart Festival." *New Orleans Times-Picayune*, 20 November 2008, New Orleans Picayune.

King, R. "Carver Theater May Rise Again as Cultural Center." *New Orleans Times-Picayune*, 18 November 1998.

Labouisse, Monroe. "The Ironical History of Armstrong Park." *New Orleans Magazine*, July 1974, 74–78.

———. "Louis Armstrong Park, Part II." *New Orleans Magazine*, August 1974, 68–73.

LaCoste, Mary. "Battling Blight and Recreating Neighborhoods." *New Orleans Tribune*, May 2001.

Lafourcade, E. "Storm of Protest Brewing over Armstrong Park Plans." *New Orleans Times-Picayune*, 12 August 1973.

Leser, D. "Park Plan Needs Study, Councilman Says." *New Orleans Times-Picayune*, 13 March 1983.

Lincoln, Ray. "Battle Lines Form over Tremé Funds." *New Orleans States-Item*, [n.d.] September 1973. Louis Armstrong Park Vertical File, Hogan Jazz Archive.

McKenna, Beverley. "There's No Place Like Home." *New Orleans Tribune*, April 2001.

McQuaid, John. "A Silent Invader Bursts into View." *New Orleans Times-Picayune*, 28 June 1998. http://www.nola.com/speced/homewreckers/day1mainstory1.html (accessed 22 March 2010).

"Modified Louis Armstrong Park Gets CPC Approval," *New Orleans Times-Picayune*, 21 November 1974.

Nolan, Bruce. "Archbishop Closes St. Augustine after Disruption of Sunday Mass." *New Orleans Times-Picayune*, 28 March 2006.

———. "Archdiocese Closes Seven Churches; Downsized Rebuilding Plan Adjusts to Katrina's Damage." *New Orleans Times-Picayune*, 10 February 2006.

———. "Parish Gets Chance to Prove Itself a Blessing." *New Orleans Times-Picayune*, 6 April 2006.

———. "St. Augustine Parish Counts Its Blessings." *New Orleans Times-Picayune*, 2 March 2009.

———. "St. Augustine Parish to Close." *New Orleans Times-Picayune*, 10 February 2006.

———. "Supporters Still in Church Rectory." *New Orleans Times-Picayune*, 22 March 2006.

Ott, D. "Officials Give Tremé Pledge." *New Orleans Times-Picayune*, 7 March 1972.

———. "Tremé Group Demands Half Cultural Center Jobs." *New Orleans Times-Picayune*, 5 March 1972.

"Paved with Good Intentions: The Casino Odyssey, from the High to the Low to the Halt of the Show." *New Orleans Times-Picayune*, 3 December 1995.

Peck, Renee. "Vieux Redo: Once a Low Rent District, the Rampart Street Edge of the Quarter Is Returning to Residential Life." *New Orleans Times-Picayune*, 25 September 2004.

Perlstein, Michael. "Chief of Chiefs Dies at Meeting." *New Orleans Times-Picayune*, 28 June 2005.

Persica, D. "Once Burned Tremé Wary of Casino." *New Orleans Times-Picayune*, 28 April 1995.

Petroski, Henry. "Raise the Ground." *New York Times*, 10 September 2005.

Pitts, L. "No Place Like Tremé." *New Orleans Gambit Weekly*, 8 August 2000.

"Police Must Patrol along Rampart." *New Orleans Times-Picayune*, 11 July 1998.

Pope, John. "Armstrong Park: Opener Swings from Politics to Jazz, and No Turning Back." *New Orleans States-Item*, 16 April 1980.

". . . Proposal Made." *New Orleans Times-Picayune*, 1 July 1972.

Quigley, Bill. "Bulldozing Hope: HUD to New Orleans' Poor: "Go F(ind) Yourself (Housing)!" 19 June 2006. http://www.counterpunch.org/quigley06192006.html (accessed 30 June 2006).

———. "New Orleans: HUD Policies Limiting Housing for Poor." 29 December 2006. http://www.truthout.org/article/bill-quigley-new-orleans-hud-policies-limiting-housing-poor?print (accessed 10 October 2008).

———. "Six Months after Katrina." 21 February 2006. www.Counterpunch.org/quigley02212006.html (accessed 21 February 2006).

———. "Tale of Two Sisters: Why Is HUD Using Tens of Millions of Katrina Money to Bulldoze 4534 Public Housing Apartments in New Orleans When It Costs Less to Repair and Open Them Up?" 29 December 2006. http://www.counterpunch.org/quigley12292006.html (accessed 5 May 2007).

Raber, R. "Ruins Road: I-10 Killed N. Claiborne." *New Orleans Times-Picayune*, 19 February 1984.

Ramsey, Jan. "North Rampart Needs a Savior." *Offbeat*, 1 June 2007, 8.

Reckdahl, Katy. "Down on the Corner." *New Orleans Gambit Weekly*, 18 May 2004, http://bestofneworleans.com/gyrobase/Content?oid=oid%3A32266 (accessed 20 May 2004).

———. "The Price of Parading: Are NOPD's Increased Parade Fees an Attempt to Stop Second Lines?" *Offbeat*, November 2006, 22.

———. "St. Joseph's Night Gone Blue." *New Orleans Gambit Weekly*, 29 March 2005, http://bestofneworleans.com/gyrobase/Content?oid=oid%3A34185 (accessed 1 May 2005).

"Residents Want Say in Park; 'No Comment,' Morial Says." Unidentified newspaper clipping, 23 July 1983. Louis Armstrong Park Vertical File, Hogan Jazz Archive.

"Restoring a Piece of Tremé History." *New Orleans Gambit Weekly*, 1 December 1998.

Ricard, U. S., Jr. "African-Americans Left Out." *New Orleans Times-Picayune*, 8 April 1990.

Richardson, Brenda. "The Battle for Louis Armstrong Park." *North Star News and Analysis: The Voice of Today's African American* 2, no. 5 (1990), 12.

Roberts, Gregory. "Movement to Enshrine Jazz Could Boost City, Tourism." *New Orleans Times-Picayune*, 8 August 1993.

Roberts, Michelle. "Archdiocese of New Orleans Shuts down Historic Black Church." Associated Press, 28 March 2006.

Ruth, Dawn. "Other Music Ideas Tuned Up for Armstrong Park." *New Orleans Times-Picayune*, 20 March 1991.

Shepard, Richard. "Lincoln Center — The First 20 Years." *New York Times*, 20 May 1979.

Simmons, Ann. "New Orleans' Fees Will Kill Jazz Funerals, Suit Says." *Los Angeles Times*. 17 November 2006. http://www.latimes.com (accessed 18 November 2008).

"Six City Bond Aims Approved," *New Orleans Times-Picayune*, 8 February 1959.

Smith, M. "Develop Park to Preserve Our Cultural Heritage." *New Orleans Times-Picayune*, 15 September 1990.

Thomas, Greg. "Grand Visions: Architect Sees Rampart Rebirth in Old Home He Plans to Convert into Eight Ritzy Condos." *New Orleans Times-Picayune*, 18 April 2003.

"Toward Bringing Back Tremé." *New Orleans Times-Picayune*, 28 November 1997.

Tucker, K. "A Memorial to Satchmo." *New Orleans Times-Picayune*, 11 April 1980.

"Use of City Funds to Buy Land Gets Unofficial OK." *New Orleans Times-Picayune*, 15 July 1964.

Ussery, Bob. "Rampart Shooting Victim Is Dead." *New Orleans Times-Picayune*, 7 October 1997.

Varney, James. "HANO Wants Only Working Tenants, Council Members Applaud Screening." *New Orleans Times-Picayune*, 21 February 2006.

———. "Unlicensed N. Rampart Clubs Fear Heat: Officer's Visit to Café Leads to Canceled Gig." *New Orleans Times-Picayune*, 14 December 2004.

Warner, C. "Armstrong Could Hum Tivoli Tune." *New Orleans Times-Picayune*, 16 October 1987.

———. "Loan OK'd to Revamp Armstrong." *New Orleans Times-Picayune*, 19 October 1990.

———. "Money Delay May Drown Plans for Armstrong Park." *New Orleans Times-Picayune*, 5 May 1990.

———. "Morial Draws up Jazz Park Plan." *New Orleans Times-Picayune*, 28 May 1996.

"Woman Slain in N.O. Park." *The Advocate*, 9 January 1987.

Wyckoff, G. "Brass Bands in the Park." *New Orleans Gambit Weekly*, 23 August 1986.

Young, T. "Man Shot, Killed at Tremé Bar." *New Orleans Times-Picayune*, 30 December 2002. http://www.nola.com/printer/printer.ssf?/newsstory/slay30.html (accessed 22 April 2008).

Plan Reports, Studies, Government Documents

Andrews and Clark, consulting engineers. *Arterial Plan for New Orleans*. 1946.

Armstrong Park Corporation. *Master Plan of Armstrong Park*. 1983.

Bureau of Governmental Research. *Wards of New Orleans*. 1961.

Claiborne Avenue Design Team. *CADT I-10 Multi-Use Study*. 197?.

Conservation Foundation. *National Parks for the Future*. 1972.

Economic Consulting Services. *Economic Evaluation of Development: The Development Potential for Armstrong Tivoli*. 1989.

Filipich, J. *Lakefront New Orleans: Planning and Development, 1926–1971*. New Orleans: Louisiana State University in New Orleans, Urban Studies Institute, 1971.

Harland Bartholomew and Associates. *A 25-Year Urban Redevelopment Program* (New Orleans). 1952.

———. *Master Plan for New Orleans*. 1951.

———. *Preliminary Report on Public Recreation Facilities in New Orleans and on Civic Art*. 1929.

Harrison Price Company. *Development Feasibility of Louis Armstrong Park, New Orleans, La.* 1982.

Jankowiak, W. *Black Social Aid and Pleasure Clubs: Marching Associations in New Orleans*. 1986.

Jerde, C., and J. Treffinger. *Jazz-Related Sites and Structures in the New Orleans Area: Final Report*. 1990.

New Orleans, City of. *Claiborne Corridor: Environmental Improvements Project Phase 1*. March 1981.

New Orleans, City of, and U.S. Department of the Interior, National Park Service. *Cooperative Agreement between the City of New Orleans and Jean Lafitte National Historical Park*. 12 March 1987.

———. *Cooperative Agreement between National Park Service and the City of New Orleans*. 8 April 1998.

New Orleans, City of, Bring New Orleans Back Commission. *Report of the Cultural Committee*. 17 January 2006.

New Orleans, City of, Mayor's Office of Communications. *Alcohol Board Revokes Permit for Joe's Cozy Corner*. 26 April 2006.

New Orleans, City of, Office of Mayoral Transition. *Special Task Force Report: Armstrong Park*. Prepared for Mayor-Elect Ernest N. Morial by Dr. Ralph Thayer. January–April 1978.

New Orleans, City of, Office of Planning and Development. *Bid Proposal for the City of New Orleans for Armstrong Park*. 7 October 1982.

New Orleans, City of, Planning Commission. *Cultural Center — (AREA #1) Part II of Application for Grant*. 1965. Excerpts of the Minutes of the Public Hearing for the Cultural Center Project, 22 July 1965.

———. *Public Buildings Report II: Cultural-International Centers*. 1960.

New Orleans, City of, Planning and Zoning Commission. *City Plan Report: Civic Art*. Prepared by Harland Bartholomew and Associates. 8 April 1931.

Shenkel, R. *Archeology of the Jazz Complex and Beauregard (Congo) Square, Louis Armstrong Park, New Orleans, Louisiana*. 1980.

Smith, M. *Economic Development and Conservation of Multi-Cultural Heritage in the Modern City: Proposal for the Development of Louis Armstrong Park as a City Park for New Orleans Music and Cultural Heritage — Including the Preservation of Jazz Park*. 1991.

Steptoe, Roosevelt, and Clarence Thornton. *The Differential Influence of an Interstate Highway on the Structure, Growth, and Development of Low-Income Minority Communities: A Comparison with Majority Communities, University Research Results*. 1986.

Tivoli International. *Master Plan: Armstrong Tivoli Park in the City of New Orleans*. 1988.

U.S. Department of the Interior. *The National Parks: Index 1997–1999*. 1997.
U.S. Department of the Interior, National Park Service. *New Orleans Jazz National Historical Park: Draft General Management Plan/Environmental Impact Statement.* 1998.
———. *New Orleans Jazz National Historical Park: Final Abbreviated General Management Plan/Environmental Impact Statement.* 1999.
———. *New Orleans Jazz Study: Louisiana: Special Resource Study: Suitability/ Feasibility Study and Study of Alternatives: Environmental Assessment.* 1993.
———. *Revision of National Park Service Thematic Framework.* 1994. http://www.nps. gov/history/history/hisnps/NPSthinking/thematic.htm (accessed spring 2000).
University of New Orleans, College of Urban and Public Affairs. *Enhancing the Sense of Place in Tremé: Mechanisms for Preserving a Unique Neighborhood.* 1995.
Wood, A. B. 1925. *Wood Screw Pumps.* Bulletin Series A. No. 2.

Theses and Dissertations

Alberts, John. "Origins of Black Catholic Parishes in the Archdiocese of New Orleans." Ph.D. diss., Louisiana State University, 1998.
Andre, James. "Urban Renewal and Housing in New Orleans, 1949–1962." Master's thesis, Louisiana State University, 1961.
Anthony, Arthé Agnes. "The Negro Creole Community in New Orleans, 1880–1920: An Oral History." Ph.D. diss., University of California, Irvine, 1978.
Cangelosi, Robert. "Which Way Tremé?" Master's thesis, Louisiana State University, 1975.
Crutcher, Michael. "Protecting 'Place' in African-American Neighborhoods: Urban Public Space, Privatization, and Protest in Louis Armstrong Park and the Tremé, New Orleans." Ph.D. diss., Louisiana State University, 2001.
Gallas, Walter. "Neighborhood Preservation and Politics in New Orleans: Vieux Carré Property Owners, Residents, and Associates, Inc., and City Government, 1938–1983." Master's thesis, University of New Orleans, 1996.
Gaudin, Wendy Ann. "Autocrats and All Saints: Migration, Memory, and Modern Creole Identities." Ph.D. diss., New York University, 2005.
Huaracha, Zella. "Evolution of a Public Open Space: From Congo Square to Armstrong Park, New Orleans, La." Master's thesis, University of New Orleans, 1994.
Irwin, Martha P. "Portrait of a Neighborhood: The Socio-Economic Status of Free People of Color and Whites in Tremé, New Orleans, Louisiana, 1810–1840." Master's thesis, University of New Orleans, 1998.
Knopp, Lawrence. "Gentrification and Gay Community Development in a New Orleans Neighborhood." Ph.D. diss., University of Iowa, 1989.
McGowan, James. "Creation of a Slave Society: Louisiana Plantations in the Eighteenth Century." Ph.D. diss., University of Rochester, 1976.

Parekh, Trushna. "Inhabiting Tremé: Gentrification, Memory, and Racialized Space in a New Orleans Neighborhood." Ph.D. diss., University of Texas at Austin, 2008.

Samuels, Daniel Robert. "Remembering North Claiborne: Community and Place in Downtown New Orleans." Master's thesis, University of New Orleans, 2000.

Video Recordings

A House Divided. New Orleans: Xavier University, n.d.

Shake the Devil Off. Directed by Peter Entell. Show and Tell Films, 2007.

INDEX

GEOGRAPHIES OF JUSTICE AND SOCIAL TRANSFORMATION

CPSIA information can be obtained
at www.ICGtesting.com
Printed in the USA
FSOW01n0349250815
10218FS

9 780820 335957